Quick Guide

SIDING

CREATIVE HOMEOWNER PRESS®

COPYRIGHT © 1995
CREATIVE HOMEOWNER PRESS®
A Division of Federal Marketing Corp.
Upper Saddle River, NJ

Quick Guide is a registered trademark of Creative Homeowner Press®

Manufactured in the United States of America

Editorial Director: David Schiff
Author: David Toht, Greenleaf Publishing, Inc.
Copy Editor: Kimberly Catanzarite
Editorial Assistant: Patrick Quinn
Art Director: Annie Jeon
Illustrator: Ed Lipinski
Production: Boultinghouse & Boultinghouse, Inc.

Cover Design: Warren Ramezzana
Cover Illustrations: Paul M. Schumm

Electronic Prepress: TBC Color Imaging, Inc.
Printed at: Quebecor Printing Inc.

Current Printing (last digit)
10 9 8 7 6 5 4 3 2

Quick Guide: Siding
LC: 94-069649
ISBN: 1-880029-40-5 (paper)

CREATIVE HOMEOWNER PRESS®
A Division of Federal Marketing Corp.
24 Park Way
Upper Saddle River, NJ 07458

CONTENTS

S A F E T Y   F I R S T

Though all the designs and methods in this book have been tested for safety, it is not possible to overstate the importance of using the safest construction methods possible. What follows are reminders; some do's and don'ts of basic carpentry. They are not substitutes for your own common sense.

■ *Always* use caution, care, and good judgment when following the procedures described in this book.

■ *Always* be sure that the electrical setup is safe; be sure that no circuit is overloaded, and that all power tools and electrical outlets are properly grounded. Do not use power tools in wet locations.

■ *Always* read container labels on paints, solvents, and other products; provide ventilation, and observe all other warnings.

■ *Always* read the tool manufacturer's instructions for using a tool, especially the warnings.

■ *Always* use holders or pushers to work pieces shorter than 3 inches on a table saw or jointer. Avoid working short pieces if you can.

■ *Always* remove the key from any drill chuck (portable or press) before starting the drill.

■ *Always* pay deliberate attention to how a tool works so that you can avoid being injured.

■ *Always* know the limitations of your tools. Do not try to force them to do what they were not designed to do.

■ *Always* make sure that any adjustment is locked before proceeding. For example, always check the rip fence on a table saw or the bevel adjustment on a portable saw before starting to work.

■ *Always* clamp small pieces firmly to a bench or other work surfaces when sawing or drilling.

■ *Always* wear the appropriate rubber or work gloves when handling chemicals, heavy construction or when sanding.

■ *Always* wear a disposable mask when working with odors, dusts or mists. Use a special respirator when working with toxic substances.

■ *Always* wear eye protection, especially when using power tools or striking metal on metal or concrete; a chip can fly off, for example, when chiseling concrete.

■ *Always* be aware that there is never time for your body's reflexes to save you from injury from a power tool in a dangerous situation; everything happens too fast. Be *alert!*

■ *Always* keep your hands away from the business ends of blades, cutters and bits.

■ *Always* hold a portable circular saw with both hands so that you will know where your hands are.

■ *Always* use a drill with an auxiliary handle to control the torque when large size bits are used.

■ *Always* check your local building codes when planning new construction. The codes are intended to protect public safety and should be observed to the letter.

■ *Never* work with power tools when you are tired or under the influence of alcohol or drugs.

■ *Never* cut very small pieces of wood or pipe. Whenever possible, cut small pieces off larger pieces.

■ *Never* change a blade or a bit unless the power cord is unplugged. Do not depend on the switch being off; you might accidentally hit it.

■ *Never* work in insufficient lighting.

■ *Never* work while wearing loose clothing, hanging hair, open cuffs, or jewelry.

■ *Never* work with dull tools. Have them sharpened, or learn how to sharpen them yourself.

■ *Never* use a power tool on a work piece that is not firmly supported or clamped.

■ *Never* saw a work piece that spans a large distance between horses without close support on either side of the kerf; the piece can bend, closing the kerf and jamming the blade, causing saw kickback.

■ *Never* support a work piece with your leg or other part of your body when sawing.

■ *Never* carry sharp or pointed tools, such as utility knives, awls, or chisels in your pocket. If you want to carry tools, use a special-purpose tool belt with leather pockets and holders.

SIDING TOOLS & MATERIALS

Having the right tools and equipment simplifies any job. Tools and materials are the vital aids that contribute to a job well done and must be selected carefully. Today there are more options for siding materials than ever before. Choose the appropriate material to suit both your style and budget.

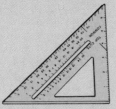

Angle Square. This handy tool can be used as a guide for trimming siding and is easily slipped into a back pocket or nail apron.

Framing Square. Designed for laying out stairs and roofs, framing squares also are used for squaring work and extending 90-degree angles.

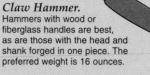

Claw Hammer. Hammers with wood or fiberglass handles are best, as are those with the head and shank forged in one piece. The preferred weight is 16 ounces.

Caulk Gun. Loaded with the proper cartridge, the caulk gun applies a consistent bead of caulk or adhesive.

Handsaw. In places where heights make it difficult or dangerous to use a power saw, use a handsaw instead.

Chalkline. A chalkline is essential for establishing alignment. It also doubles as a plumb bob.

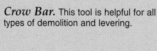

Drill Bit Set. Have on hand a selection of smaller-dimension drill bits for drilling pilot holes and applying pop rivets.

Hand Stapler. Although not as fast as the hammer tacker, the hand stapler also can be used for installing building or tar paper. Use it when staples must be accurately positioned.

Line Level. A small level that hangs on a string, a line level is useful for checking for level over long distances.

Crow Bar. This tool is helpful for all types of demolition and levering.

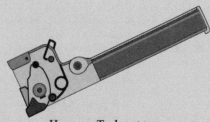

Hammer Tacker. A hammer tacker is the fastest way to install building or tar paper. It drives staples simply by striking the surface.

Chisel. Use this tool to remove damaged wood.

Circular Saw. Equipped with a crosscut blade for framing, a combination blade for wood siding, or a plywood blade for sheathing, a 7 1/4-inch circular saw is indispensable.

Keyhole Saw. This saw has a long blade and is ideal for cutting awkward areas.

Sliding T-Bevel. This tool has an adjustable bar that matches the angle of a cut for easy transfer to another piece of wood.

Scribing Compass. A simple grade-school compass is perfect for transferring complex profiles.

Nail Apron. A canvas apron is essential for holding nails, utility knife and hammer. These are tools you constantly use while siding.

Putty Knife. Use this tool to spread putty, and to smooth caulk and epoxy repair compound.

Pry Bar. The pry bar is preferred over thicker crowbars for getting underneath siding. It is helpful for repairs and tear-off jobs.

Spirit Level. The spirit level is used to check that siding is vertically or horizontally true.

Cat's Paw. Used in rough work, the cat's paw can extract nails from below the surface of the wood.

Saber Saw. Complex cuts are made with the plunging blade of this tool.

Pop Riveter. Indispensable when working with aluminum siding, this tool joins metal sheets with rivets that are available in a variety of sizes.

Power Drill. This tool is necessary when applying flashing and drilling pilot holes. Cordless varieties offer convenience well worth the cost.

Tin Snips. This scissors-like tool cuts flashing and aluminum siding.

Utility Knife. Also called a razor knife, this handy tool is used for everything from cutting synthetic building paper to trimming wood shingles.

Tape Measure. A flexible tape measure is an essential tool. A 25 or 50-foot reel is worth the investment.

Ladders

Nothing is more tedious than climbing up and down a ladder just to move it a bit this way or that as your work proceeds. However, the dangerous alternative to moving the ladder is leaning uncomfortably far to the left or right just to hammer a nail home. Face it, the job of repairing or replacing siding involves working high above the ground, and since you have to be up there, you may as well have a safe, generous platform upon which to work. This—along with, common sense, the appropriate tools and a few precautions—will get you through the job safely.

Ladders. Use a ladder that is rated Type I (heavy duty, capable of bearing 250 pounds per rung). Wooden ladders are less likely to slide on a gutter or be blown over, and they do not conduct electricity, unless wet. However, they are heavy and difficult to move unless you have assistance. Aluminum ladders are easy to move but they conduct electricity and may be blown down or knocked over. Expensive fiberglass ladders are relatively light and are nonconductive. Make sure your ladder is at least 15 inches wide with rungs that are 12 inches apart. The best of them have nonskid feet, rope-and-pulley extension mechanisms and padded safety-wall grips.

Safe Placement. The angle at which the ladder leans against the house is very important. If the angle is too great the ladder is subject to strain and may break or bend. If the angle is too small the ladder is likely to fall backward. Position the ladder so that the feet are at least one foot from the house for every four feet the ladder is extended.

Make sure the ladder is level. If the ground is so soft that a leg of the ladder might sink and cause it to tip to one side, set the ladder on a piece of plywood.

Be sure the ladder extends 3 feet above the edge of the roof to permit a firm grip as you step onto the roof. Climb onto a roof from the eaves side only—never over a gable. Move the ladder frequently rather than trying to reach by leaning.

Safe Climbing. Always face forward and keep your hips within the rails of the ladder. Allow only one person on the ladder at a time. As a precaution, thoroughly sweep the area in which you are working and wear shoes that have rubber soles.

Caution: *Always be aware of the location of electrical lines particularly when moving a ladder. An aluminum or wet wooden ladder is conductive and can transmit a fatal shock.*

Ladders. Use a ladder that is at least 15 in. wide with 12 in. between rungs.

Safe Placement. Before climbing make sure the ladder is level and has a secure base. Shim the ladder if the ground is not level (left). Firemen extend the ladder at arm's length as shown to determine a safe angle to lean the ladder.

Brackets, Jacks & Scaffolding

Adequate scaffolding and working platforms make a siding job quicker and safer and can be rented for the duration of a job. There are a variety of brackets, jacks and scaffolding from which to choose. They range from simple metal roof cleats for working on dormers to full-fledged pipe scaffolding which provides plenty of working space.

Ladder Jacks. Consider using ladder jacks for working under eaves or when applying siding. They are attached to the top of the ladder or slung underneath and can support a 2×10 work platform up to 9 feet long.

Pump Jacks. These movable platform supports are raised and lowered to suit the task. When you pump the lever with your foot they ride up and down a pair of doubled 2×4s. You can add accessory brackets to make a handy elevated workbench. Pump jacks also operate as freight elevators for raising large or heavy objects.

High Horses. Portable high horses are great for first-story work. Build them so the middle support bar is level with the height of your lower sawhorses. Doing this provides you with two working areas and easy access to the upper platform.

Scaffolding. Pipe scaffolding is set up alongside the house. With a deck made of 2×4s and construction-grade plywood, this structure provides a spacious work area. Use scraps of wood to level the scaffold and keep the legs from sinking into soft ground. Keep the uprights perpendicular to the ground and the platforms level. If the scaffold is taller than 12 feet secure it to the wall.

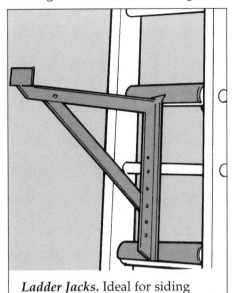

Ladder Jacks. Ideal for siding work, jacks move and adjust easily.

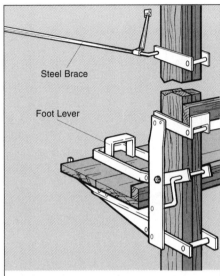

Steel Brace

Foot Lever

Pump Jacks. Pump jacks ride up and down on doubled 2×4s set vertically.

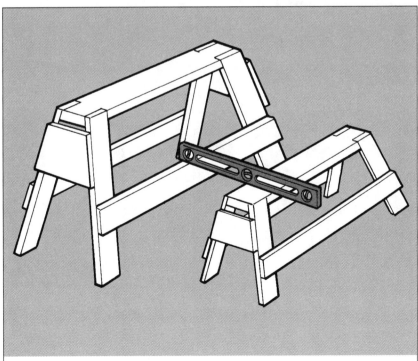

High Horses. Two-level horses are easy to make and can be useful in many circumstances.

Scaffolding. The best platform of all is pipe scaffolding.

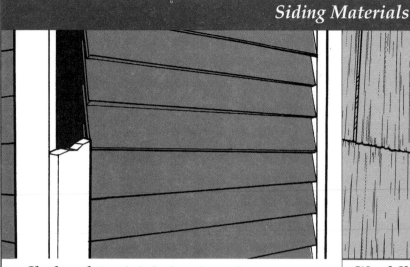

Clapboard. Beveled clapboards are the most common type of wood siding and can be found in a variety of horizontal styles.

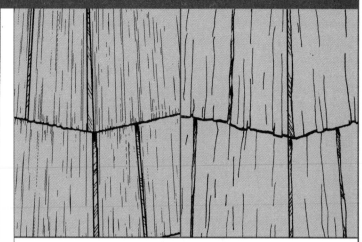

Wood Shingles and Shakes. Shingles (left) are more regular than shakes (right). Both are durable, but slow to install and expensive.

Hardboard Siding. Planks and sheets are inexpensive, long lasting and available in many textures including stucco. Its heavier weight complicates installation.

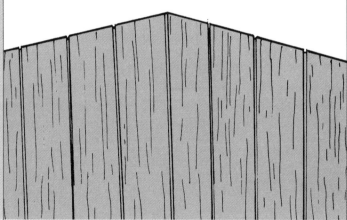

Plywood Siding. As panels or planks, plywood siding is relatively light, strong and affordable. The process of sealing and maintenance is important with this material.

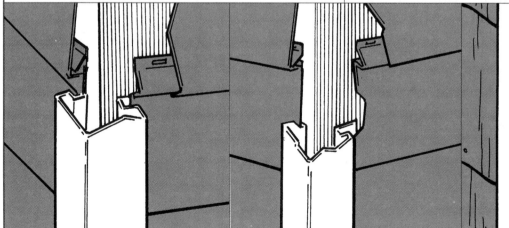

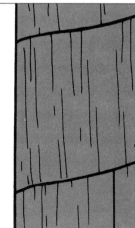

Vinyl Siding. Available in a wide variety of colors, with matching trim and architectural details.

Aluminum Siding. Quickly applied and requires little initial maintenance. Dents and scratches easily.

Fiber-Reinforced Cement Siding. Different styles and textures never rot or degrade, but pieces may crack.

REPAIRING SIDING

Damage to siding often is localized. Commonly wood clapboards split at corners and develop moisture damage due to faulty gutters, rotting drip caps or ground splash. Other types of siding suffer local damage as well. Wood shingles crack and loosen, aluminum dents, vinyl splits and fiber-reinforced shingles shatter. Spot repairs can be done in such a way that they blend into the healthy siding that remains.

Repairing Wood Clapboard Siding

Damage to wood clapboard siding ranges from small splits at siding joints to major areas of rot. Replacing sections of siding is a slow process that is well worth the effort as long as it prevents you from having to replace entire walls of siding. Clapboard siding is installed with each nail piercing only one piece of siding.

Replacing a Clapboard

1 Avoiding Chips. If the siding has been painted score along overlaps and at joints along the trim on the damaged board to avoid paint chips on the "healthy" boards that will remain.

2 Pulling Back the Overlap. Remove the nails above the damaged board by inserting a pry bar under the siding directly under each nail. Pry outward until the nails come loose 1/4 inch.

3 Removing the Nails. Swat the siding back down so the nail head sticks up. Do this by hammering on the end of a pry bar to avoid denting the overlapping siding. Use a thin scrap of wood or a putty knife as a cushion and pry out the nail. Release the bottom of the damaged board using the same procedure.

4 Marking a Cut Line. If you do not need to replace the entire piece of siding, a section can be cut. Make the cut over a stud. This provides a nailing surface for the new joint. Then remove the nails from the area to be cut. Measure between the approximate on-center points of the two studs. Cut a piece of replacement siding to fit. Lay the replacement piece on the damaged area and use a utility knife to scribe lines on the damaged area.

Wall Stud

Repairing Wood Clapboard Siding. Each nail is driven through one clapboard only. This nail goes just above the clapboard below.

1 Use a utility knife to score between siding courses. This helps avoid paint chips.

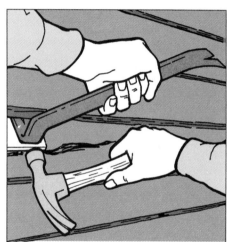

2 Tap the end of a pry bar under the clapboard above the damage. Allow nails to give 1/4 in.

3 Swat back the siding while protecting the wood with the flat end of the pry bar. Pull the nails.

Replacement Piece

4 To remove a piece of siding, mark a cut line over a wall stud.

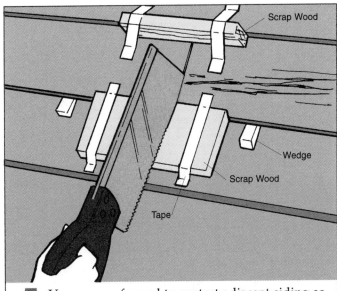

Scrap Wood

Wedge

Scrap Wood

Tape

5 Use scraps of wood to protect adjacent siding as you cut the damaged siding with a backsaw.

6 Work the end of a keyhole saw under the overlapping siding and finish the cut.

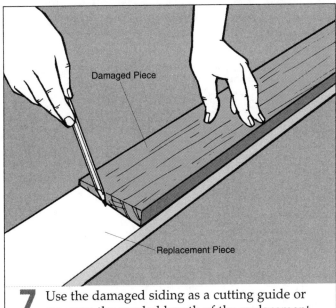

Damaged Piece

Replacement Piece

7 Use the damaged siding as a cutting guide or measure the needed length of the replacement.

8 Measure exposure as you tap the replacement piece into place.

5 Cutting the Siding. Cut with a backsaw, being careful not to damage the siding above the repair. (The backsaw has teeth that are fine enough to make a neat cut.) Use wedges to separate damaged siding.

6 Completing the Cut. Use a keyhole saw to complete the cut beneath the upper piece of siding. Once both ends of the damaged siding are released the other nails can be removed.

7 Replacing the Damage. Prime both sides of the replacement siding before installing. Measure the necessary length or use the damaged piece of siding as a guide. Use a combination or fine-cut circular saw blade or a fine-toothed handsaw to cut the siding to length. Slip the siding under the course above it (you may need a helper to do this). The best fit is a snug one; no more than a 1/16-inch gap (to be caulked) at both ends.

8 Nailing the Replacement. To avoid creating cracks when nailing, drill a pilot hole slightly smaller than the nail shank, or blunt the point of the nail by tapping it with a hammer. Use hot-dipped galvanized 8d box nails. Each nail pierces only one layer of siding, typically an inch or more above the bottom edge. Measure the exposure as you tap the siding into place.

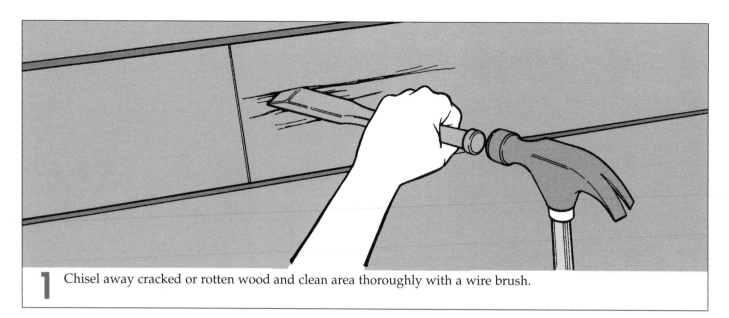

1 Chisel away cracked or rotten wood and clean area thoroughly with a wire brush.

Patching Wood Siding with Epoxy

Some siding repairs do not require the removal of siding. When damage is localized (around a rusty nail or next to the trim) and the siding is otherwise sound, save on costly material by doing a spot repair. Two-part epoxy-based patching compounds are available to fill punctured or rotted areas of siding.

1 **Removing the Damage.** Chisel out the face of the board to remove loose or rotten wood. Dig deep enough to find sound wood. Then clean the area with a wire brush.

2 **Combining Epoxy.** Mix the two parts as directed. Two applications may be necessary if the hole is deep. If the hole is located along the edge of the siding, cover a piece of scrap wood with thin plastic (so it releases from the epoxy later) and use it as a mold by tacking it to the siding. Make sure the final layer is as smooth and even as possible to save yourself filing and sanding time later.

3 **Smoothing the Area.** Once thoroughly dry, smooth the area with a wood file or rasp. Sand and prime before painting.

2 Mix the compound and press it firmly into the hole. A scrap of wood covered with thin plastic helps maintain a clean bottom edge.

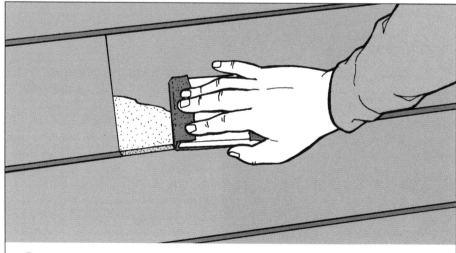

3 File, sand and prime the patch before painting.

Repairing Tongue-and-Groove Siding

Like clapboard siding, tongue-and-groove siding is installed with each nail penetrating only one piece. The nails are driven at an angle. Tongue-and-groove siding is more difficult to repair than clapboard because it does not pry off easily. The pieces being replaced must be cut off in such a way that the pieces above and below are not damaged.

1 Cutting the Damage. Determine the area you want to replace and mark cut lines at wall studs. (Look for nailheads to locate studs.) Nails are driven into the tongues and covered by grooves, so you may have to dig at the damaged area with a chisel to locate the studs. Use a cat's paw nail puller to dig out nails. Mark cut lines outside where the cat's paw dug in, but still over the studs. Use a circular saw with a combination blade to make a plunge cut. Use a 1- to 2-inch wood chisel to extend the cuts to where the sawblade couldn't reach.

2 Splitting the Damage. Make a horizontal plunge cut midway up the damaged area.

3 Removing a Section. Use a hammer and chisel to complete the split. Pull the loosened board away, prying at the horizontal cut if necessary. Check the building paper for tears and repair them with a scrap of tar paper or roofing cement.

4 Replacing the Board. Cut a piece of tongue-and-groove siding to the proper length. With a chisel, circular saw or table saw, remove the back edge of the groove. Insert the tongue in the plank above the damaged area and push the replacement piece into place. Drill 1/16-inch pilot holes at the ends of the replacement board and nail with 8d galvanized nails. Set the nails and putty the set holes before painting.

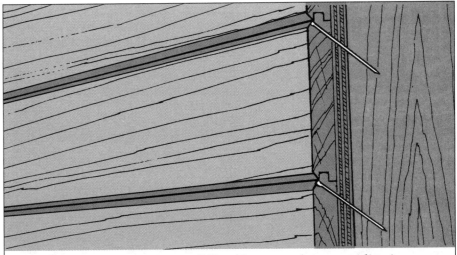

Repairing Tongue-and-Groove Siding. Tongue-and-groove siding is more difficult to repair and replace than clapboard because the courses interlock.

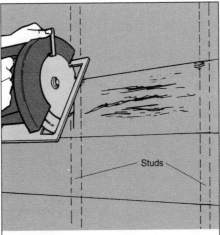

Studs

1 Use a circular saw to make plunge cuts. Finish the cuts using a chisel.

2 Use the circular saw to cut horizontally through the center of the damaged section.

3 Split the wood and pry the pieces outward. Repair tears in the building paper.

4 Cut away back edge of the groove on replacement. Drill pilot holes and nail at studs.

Repairing Wood Shingles

Shingles are installed in either single or double courses. Like clapboards, single-coursed shingles are fastened simply with nails driven directly into them. If the shingles are double-coursed, the nailheads are exposed and each nail pierces four shingles. In either case, the most difficult step is removing old nails without damaging adjacent shingles. Wood shingles added to walls that are not painted or sealed "weather in" after a few months and eventually match the surrounding color.

1 **Removing the Damage.** Many things contribute to the deterioration of shingles on exterior walls:

impact, dampness, prolonged exposure to sun and old age. Use a wood chisel or the sharp end of a pry bar to split a damaged shingle in several places. Pull out the split pieces and remove the nails that secured the damaged shingles.

2 **Removing Remaining Nails.** By removing the damaged shingle, some space is created along the length of the nails in the good shingle above. If you are dealing with double-coursed shingles put a block of wood against the good shingle and whack it, pushing down on the shingle. This may allow you to get the claw of a hammer or pry bar under the nailhead without digging into and damaging the good shingle. If so, protect the good shingle with a

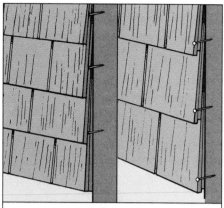

Repairing Wood Shingles. Single-coursed shingling nails penetrate one shingle (left). Double-coursed nails penetrate four shingles (right).

thin shingle scrap and pull out the nails. Otherwise you have to remove the nails by cutting them with a mini-hacksaw slipped under the good shingle. Removing the damaged shingle will free the undercourse shingle below. If the undercourse shingle is not damaged, save it for reuse. If you are dealing with single coursing the nailheads are not exposed so you have to use the mini-hacksaw.

3 **Fitting a Replacement.** Cut a replacement piece that is about 1/8 inch narrower than the space you need to fill. Use a handsaw to cut it, or score it repeatedly with a utility knife and then break it. Smooth the edge with a block plane if necessary.

1 Use a 1- to 2-in. chisel to split the damaged shingles. Then pull out the pieces.

2 Tap down the shingle to pry out the nail in double courses. Place a scrap of damaged shingle under the pry bar to protect the shingle above. For single-coursed shingles, use a mini-hacksaw to cut the hidden nails.

3 Hold the replacement piece against the wall and mark it to fit the space minus about 1/8 in.

4 **Nailing the Replacement.**
If you are replacing a double-coursed shingle, first reinstall the underlayment you saved. Install the shingle with 6d galvanized nails. Renail the shingle above. You can use the old nailholes but you will have to use galvanized nails that are slightly larger than the originals (try using 8d nails).

Single coursing requires that you hide the nails. Use 6d galvanized box nails toenailed in just below the course line. Hold the shingle about 1/4 inch below its course line while nailing. With a block, tap upward to force nailheads under the course above.

4 For single coursing, toenail 6d galvanized nails at the course line (left). Tap shingle upward to push nailheads under the course above (right).

Repairing Fiber-Reinforced Cement Shingles

Now that these shingles are made without asbestos, it is rare to find a job that entails an entire replacement. If you are contemplating a complete replacement job however, the shingles probably are old enough to contain asbestos and must be removed by professionals who have a permit to properly dispose of the material. While fiber-reinforced cement shingles do not rot and are virtually immune to the effects of weather, they are brittle. An errant line drive baseball can easily shatter this type of shingle. As a result, there may be occasion to replace individual shingles.

1 **Removing Damaged Shingles.**
Because the shingles are brittle and inflexible you will not be able to remove the nails holding the damaged shingle. Break the damaged shingle if necessary. Use a hacksaw blade to cut the nails in the upper course.

2 **Replacing Shingles.** To cut replacement shingles, first score the cut line. Use a straight-edge as a guide, while making several passes with a utility knife. Cut the replacement shingles with a circular saw equipped with a carborundum blade or, if available, rent a shingle breaker. Use a 1/8-inch masonry bit to drill holes, or pierce holes with the breaker. Then face-nail replacement shingles with 3d galvanized box nails.

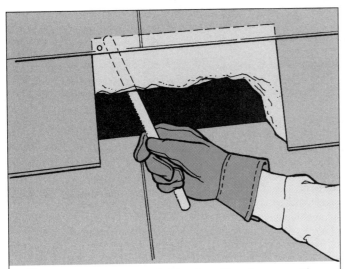

1 Break the damaged shingle with a hammer if necessary to gain acccess to the nails under the course above. Cut the nails with a hacksaw blade.

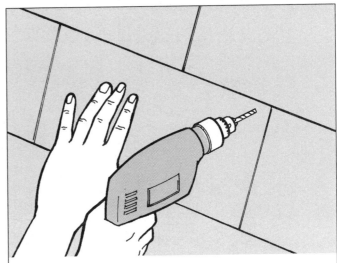

2 Use a 1/8-inch masonry bit to predrill nail holes in the replacement shingle.

Repairing Vinyl Siding

Vinyl often cracks under impact. This is true especially at low temperatures. Small cracks are patched by removing the damaged piece, cleaning the crack with PVC primer and gluing a patch of scrap siding from behind with PVC cement. If large areas are damaged the entire piece may be replaced. Vinyl siding fades with time, so your patch or replacement piece may not be a perfect color match and vinyl cannot be painted.

Each course of vinyl locks into the course below or beside it. The siding is nailed through a flange that is molded into the top of each course. A simple tool, called a zip tool, is needed to unlock the courses. This device wedges under the lower edge of siding and is pulled horizontally to unlock the pieces. When working with vertical siding the zip tool is pulled down the seam.

1 Detaching the Damaged Siding. Use the zip tool to free the damaged piece from the course below or beside it. Expose the nailing flange by freeing the course above from the damaged piece. Pull the nails and remove the damaged piece.

2 Patching or Replacing. Cut a patch larger than the crack. Coat the patch and siding with clear PVC primer, and glue it to the back of the siding with PVC cement. You also can purchase a piece of replacement siding and, using the damaged piece as a guide, cut it to size with a utility knife.

3 Replacing the Siding. Lock the lower edge in place. Then pull up the overlapping piece and nail it through the center of each flange slot. Use corrosion-resistant nails that penetrate at least 3/4 inch into sheathing. Nailheads must be a minimum of 5/16 inch in diameter. Do not hammer the nail home; it must be loose enough to allow for movement due to temperature changes.

4 Relocking the Overlap. Lock the overlapping piece by engaging the zip tool, levering the piece downward, and releasing it back into the channel.

Types of Vinyl Siding

Vinyl siding may be installed vertically or horizontally. The most common type of vinyl siding resembles two courses of wooden clapboards. Other types resemble single clapboards.

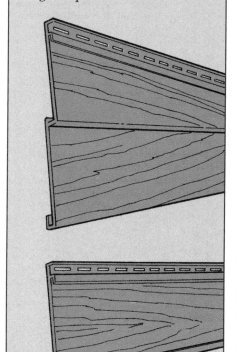

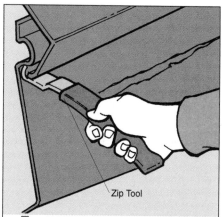

1 Pry downward as you drag the tool sideways to unlock adjacent pieces.

Zip Tool

2 Prime and cement patch from behind. If damage is severe, cut a replacement piece.

3 Lock the bottom edge of the siding and nail. Leave 1/8 in. between the nailhead and vinyl.

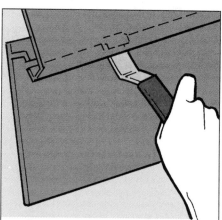

4 Relock the bottom edge of the above piece with the top edge of the replacement siding.

Repairing Aluminum Siding

Aluminum siding is a good insulator that is easy to maintain. It can be damaged, however, by a stray baseball or serious hail storm. Slight damage can be repaired. Pieces that suffer from more serious damage must be replaced. The procedure for repairing dents in aluminum siding is similar to the technique used to repair a dented car fender.

1 **Drilling Holes.** Begin by drilling 1/8-inch holes in the damaged area of the siding.

2 **Pulling out the Dent.** Insert one or more #8 sheet metal screws into the holes. Grab the screwheads with pliers and pull out the dent.

3 **Patching the Dent.** Remove the screws and sand the dented area. If creases are 1/8 inch deep or deeper, apply two-part auto body putty. Use auto body filler for very slight imperfections.

4 **Sanding and Painting.** Once the surface is dry, sand, prime, and paint it with a spray can of matching color. (If you know the manufacturer and color of the siding, you can purchase proprietary colors.)

Replacing Aluminum Siding

Because aluminum is not flexible like vinyl entire replacement pieces are not easily installed. If the area of

1 Drill several 1/8-in. holes at the deepest part of the dent.

2 Use sheet-metal screws to grab and pull out siding.

3 Mix two-part auto body filler and smooth it onto the dented area.

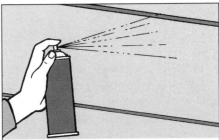

4 When patch is hard, sand and apply at least two coats of aluminum siding paint.

damage is large, cut out and replace the entire section. If you are fortunate some extra pieces of siding are squirreled away in your garage. If not, look for a siding distributor who can match the color you need and sell you just a piece or two.

1 **Cutting away Damage.** Use a utility knife to cut away the damaged area, leaving at least a 1-inch lip along the upper edge. (This will be used for gluing the replacement siding in place with caulking compound.) The replacement piece must overlap the existing siding by 3 inches at both vertical edges.

2 **Cutting the Patch.** Cut a patch long enough to overlap both sides of the area by 3 inches. Use a utility knife or tin snips to trim the nailing strip from the replacement piece. The patch will be just wide enough to fit snugly into the course above.

3 **Gluing the Patch.** Run a thick bead of butyl caulk just beneath the bottom edge of the course above and in places where the edges of the patch overlap the original siding. Lock the bottom edge of the patch into the section below. Tape it firmly in place until dry.

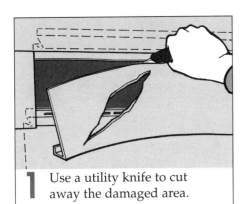

1 Use a utility knife to cut away the damaged area.

2 Trim the nailing strip from the replacement piece.

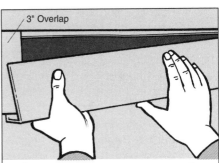

3" Overlap

3 Apply a bead of butyl caulk, and press the piece into place.

Replacing Plywood or Hardboard Panels

Small punctures and rotted areas of plywood siding are patched with epoxy compound (see page 14). Major damage or veneer failure requires that you remove the entire panel. (Major damage often is a result of faulty gutters, open seams around doors and windows, and ground splash.) Similarly hardboard panels fail if left unpainted or exposed to dampness.

Typical plywood or hardboard panels are 1/2-inch thick. Check the thickness needed before purchasing a replacement. Standard panel dimension is 4x8 feet. Before installing the panels prime them with a primer that is compatible with the final finish to be used. Panels must be finished to protect them from the weather. Paint or stain the replacement panel as soon as possible.

1 Removing the Damaged Panel. Use a utility knife to score all caulked areas along the upper and lower trim. Remove battens (if any). Then use a cat's paw to remove all nails except for two that hold the panel in place (until you are ready to remove it). If a crow bar is needed to release the seams, use only the damaged panel as a fulcrum. Pry the panel loose while an assistant holds it and takes it down.

2 Cutting a Replacement. If a full panel is removed there is no need to cut. If the old panel was cut to end a wall or fit around a window or door opening, use it as a template to lay out cuts on the new panel. When cutting, support the panel by laying two 2x4s across the sawhorses. Check the building paper for damage and patch it as warranted. Seal all edges of the panel.

3 Nailing a Replacement. Use 8d nails to install the replacement. Caulk the seams along the trim and apply the finish as soon as possible.

1 Use a cat's paw to remove all but a couple of nails at the top. While an assistant holds the panel, use a crow bar to release the last nails.

2 Use the damaged piece as a template to lay out cuts on the back of the new panel. Cut with a circular saw fitted with a plywood blade.

3 Use 8d galvanized nails to install the new piece. Caulk the seams.

PREPARING WALLS FOR NEW SIDING

A smooth surface that is covered with building paper and free from rotten or cracked sheathing not only makes for a long-lasting job but also speeds the process of siding. Take this opportunity to repair drip caps, windowsills and trim. A well-prepared job results in a fresh, new exterior.

Installing New Siding

If the old siding must be removed, you have a large job on your hands. However, if you are adding a layer of vinyl or aluminum siding over an old layer of siding, then the job is a small one. Once you have decided upon the type of siding to be used, you must provide a sound, even surface according to the requirements of that particular siding.

Remove the siding if it is very deteriorated. It is more trouble to fill voids and soft spots than it is to remove the siding completely. However, sometimes a complete tear-off job is not necessary. For example, if the old siding is relatively even and holds nails, the vinyl or aluminum siding is applied directly. You also may be able to add furring strips to provide nailers for panels or shingles.

If you remove the old siding all old nails must be removed or hammered flat. Remove building paper or felt. The following materials are needed for the job: sturdy dropcloths, hammer, pry bar, crow bar and a rented dumpster.

Caution: *Wear eye protection and a face mask.*

Repairing Sheathing

After the old siding is removed check for damage to the sheathing. It may be plywood, fiberboard, tongue-and-groove planks or planks with lap joints (called shiplap). If the house is very old you may find rubble fill or even nothing at all under the siding. If so, add insulation and consider adding sheathing as well.

Damage is most likely to occur in areas exposed to water. Check beneath eaves, in corners behind gutter downspouts and in places where the siding overlaps the foundation. Also, check the sheathing beneath windowsills.

1 Checking the Damage. Look for discoloration. Pierce darkened wood with a screwdriver. Soft or seriously cracked sheathing must be replaced.

2 Planning the Replacement. Find the studs that are nearest to both sides of the damaged area. Remove the nails with a cat's paw nail puller. Mark a vertical cutting line at the nailholes so the replacement piece can be nailed to the framing. Mark horizontal cutting lines well above and below the damaged area.

3 Cutting away Damage. Mark a cutting line and set the circular saw blade 1/8 inch deeper than the thickness of the sheathing. Make a plunge cut along the cutting line. Cut around the damaged area.

4 Adding New Sheathing. Cut the sheathing and nail it in place. It must be the same thickness as the damaged piece.

1 Remove old siding and check for rotted sheathing.

2 Remove the nails in the studs with a cat's paw nail puller.

3 Use a circular saw to cut away damaged wood.

4 Cut the sheathing and nail it in place.

Preparing Trim & Fittings

1 Stripping the Trim. When adding a new layer of siding you may need to remove the trim and thicken it so it will stand out further than the new siding. Use a flat pry bar to pry off molding and other trim. Slip the flat end of the bar under the trim and tap with a hammer to break the paint seal.

2 Building Window Casings. The new siding sticks out beyond existing window and door casings. By adding a slat to the side of a brick mold, the casing can be extended in depth up to 1 inch.

3 Clearing the Deck. Remove all fixtures and attachments including downspouts, molding and trim, and shutters and light fixtures, prior to installing the trim. Cable, phone and electrical lines also may have to be repositioned—these are not jobs to do yourself—call a utility company.

1 Remove old trim where it overlaps siding.

2 Use a 1x3 or 1x4 set on edge to extend the casings.

3 Remove gutter downspouts, shutters and other fixtures.

Furring Old Siding

Furring strips are used to avoid a tear-off. They provide a solid nailing surface. They also provide the advantage of allowing you to shim out irregularities in the walls.

1 Nailing Furring Strips. Use the location of nailheads to determine the location of studs. Cut 1x2 or 1x3 furring strips to length and nail in place. Typically, 8d common cement-coated sinkers are used, but be sure the nail penetrates at least 3/4 inch into the framing. Nail every 12 inches. If you plan to install vertical siding, place furring strips horizontally at 16-inch intervals. For horizontal siding use vertical furring.

2 Shimming Gaps. If there are obvious indentations or warps in the original siding, provide an even surface by shimming with two wood shingles. Place the shingles behind the furring, thin end over thick end. Push them together over each other to fill in the void behind the furring strip.

3 Adding a Starter Strip. To set the first course at the proper angle for horizontal siding, add a starter strip that is approximately as thick as the top edge of the siding. A piece of lattice often fits the bill.

1 Furring strips provide a solid, straight nailing surface for new siding.

2 Use wood shingles to shim out warps in the wall.

3 A strip of lattice is used for accurately setting the first course of beveled siding.

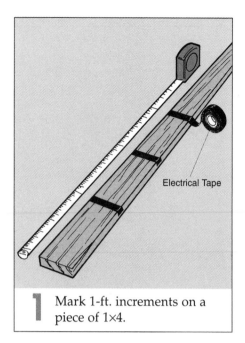

1 Mark 1-ft. increments on a piece of 1×4.

Estimating Materials

A handy way to estimate the amount of materials needed for siding is to make a boldly-marked measuring stick and lean it against the wall. Then photograph the wall, repeating the process for each wall of your home. The resulting photographs are used to estimate dimensions. They also become a ready reference for ordering materials.

1 Making a Measuring Stick. Mark a 10-foot piece of 1×4 with electrical tape every 12 inches.

2 Getting the Picture. Lean the measuring stick against each wall and take photographs.

3 Taking the Measurements. Once the photos are processed, count the markings from the comfort of your desk. Transfer the marks to an index card to make a "ruler" and use it to determine both the height and width of the wall. These photographs are a handy guide to determining how much drip edge, trim and paint you need. Keep the photographs on file for future reference.

4 Determining Wall Area. To determine square footage, walls are broken into rectangles, squares, triangles—and in the case of gambrel end walls—trapezoids. Then they are calculated accordingly. Add 10 percent to allow for errors and minor miscalculations.

2 Photograph each wall straight on. Use color print film.

3 Transfer the measuring stick marks to an index card.

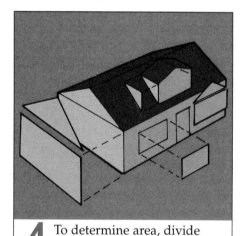

4 To determine area, divide walls into geometric shapes.

Calculating Area

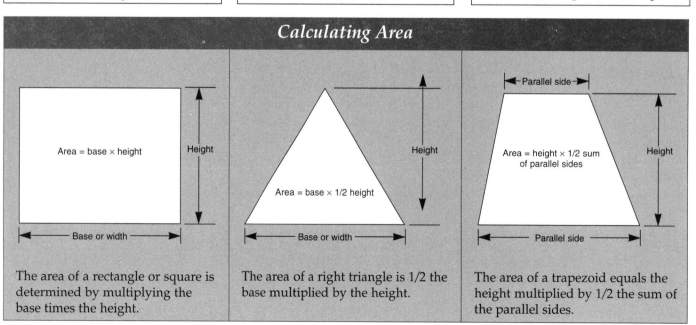

The area of a rectangle or square is determined by multiplying the base times the height.

The area of a right triangle is 1/2 the base multiplied by the height.

The area of a trapezoid equals the height multiplied by 1/2 the sum of the parallel sides.

Preparing the Walls

Before adding new siding, you may want to add insulation and/or building wrap. Both the cost and the difficulty of the job is moderate and well worth doing before adding new siding. There are several approaches that can be taken: panel insulation, blown-in insulation and building wrap.

Installing Panel Insulation

Rigid foam core panels can be added over old siding, over sheathing, or, if the studs are exposed, in the wall cavity. If you are depending on thickness, the panels add an insulation value of up to R 6.5 per inch. Panels are available as thin as 1/4 inch and are faced with reflective foil. It makes sense, however, to add the insulation value of 3/8- to 1-inch panels if you are going through the trouble of insulating.

Note: When adding insulation over sheathing or siding you may have difficulty matching new siding to old trim. This is especially true around windows and doors because of the added thickness of the panels. (See page 23 for how to build out window casings to solve this problem.)

1 Cutting Panels. Use a utility knife to cut rigid insulation board. Guide the knife with a metal yardstick or a metal drywall T-square to quickly cut panels.

2 Nailing Rigid Insulation. Use galvanized roofing nails that penetrate at least 1 inch into studs. When applying panels over beveled siding be careful to add nails into the high or butt edge of siding courses. This prevents nailing over a void and cracking the surface of the panel. Nail up the sheet at 12-inch intervals. Leave a slight gap at corners so interior vapor can escape.

1 Use a straightedge and utility knife to cut the panels.

2 Use galvanized roofing nails to nail into the high points of the siding underneath. Nail at 12-in. intervals

Vapor Symptoms & Solutions

Aluminum, like vinyl, is impermeable to water vapor. This quality is great for keeping out exterior moisture. Unfortunately, it also means that damaging moisture may become trapped within walls and insulation. To prevent this problem, new homes are built with a vapor barrier installed between the drywall and the studs. This barrier prevents interior moisture from reaching the siding. Homes built prior to the 1960s often lack this barrier. In fact, the peeling paint that inspired you to consider new siding for your home may have resulted from the lack of a vapor barrier.

Trapped moisture promotes the growth of rot and fungi and reduces the effect of existing insulation. Depending on your particular circumstances, there are different ways to deal with the problem:

■ Exhaust humid air with ventilating fans.
■ Create weep holes in siding.
■ Install soffit vents.

Installing Loose-Fill Insulation

Bags of loose-fill insulation and the blower necessary for its installation are available at lumberyards and home center stores. The blower forces insulation through a vacuum-cleaner-like hose and blows it into the walls. Usually the job requires that you remove a section of siding, cut into the wall cavity with a hole saw, blow in the material and cap the hole with a plastic cover. Some types of home construction (balloon framing in particular) allow easier access. The application of new siding is an excellent opportunity to add loose-fill insulation and easily cover up the access holes.

Note: Loose-fill insulation compacts over the years and as a result its insulation value diminishes. However, it remains a worthwhile solution when you consider the alternative (pulling off sheathing and adding batts of fiberglass).

1 Drilling Insulation Holes.
Using a 2- to 3-inch hole saw (the hole must be big enough to easily insert the blower's nozzle), cut holes just below the eaves line. Locate each hole at the center of each wall cavity.

2 Checking for Barriers. Use a plumb bob or a weight on the end of a string to determine the locations of fire stops (pieces of framing that form horizontal barriers in the framing) or other obstructions. In addition, you will find plumbing pipes, electrical wires, heating ducts and wall plates between stories. Bore additional holes beneath these barriers.

3 Adding the Insulation. The most common loose-fill insulation is cellulose (chopped and fluffed paper treated with a fire retardant). Fish the hose through the hole until it hits the bottom of the cavity. Slowly pull the hose upward as the cavity fills. Plug the holes with plastic caps or wads of fiberglass.

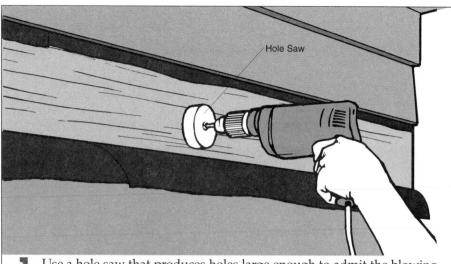

Hole Saw

1 Use a hole saw that produces holes large enough to admit the blowing equipment nozzle. Drill holes in each wall cavity along the eaves.

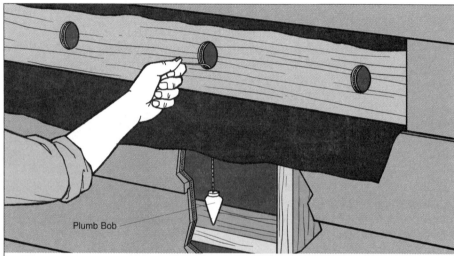

Plumb Bob

2 A plumb bob helps locate obstructions in the wall. Drill additional holes beneath each obstruction.

3 Fish the equipment nozzle into the cavity until it hits the bottom. Pull it out as insulation fills the wall.

Installing Building Wrap

Building wrap is an improvement on the old red builder's paper and tar paper. Because it stops air, but not moisture, this material allows the house to exhale moisture (thereby protecting interior insulation from condensation). At the same time, it cuts drafts and cold seep-age that creeps through exteriors, especially at corners and around openings.

1 Stapling Wrap. Building wrap is attached with staples. The horizontal overlap is 2 inches.

2 Overlapping New Rolls. When adding a new roll leave a vertical overlap of 6 inches. If the siding is not going to be installed right away, add temporary furring strips to protect wrap from being torn by the wind.

3 Wrapping the Corners. Overlap inside and outside corners 6 inches each way for complete coverage of a vulnerable area.

1 Staple wrap in place, overlapping each row by 2 in.

2 A new roll begins with a vertical overlap of 6 in.

3 Overlap corners with at least 6 in. of material.

Adding Drip Caps

If you are going to the trouble of repairing or replacing siding make sure the drip caps and windows are in good shape. Drip caps shed water from the top of window and door moldings. Some are made of wood, but recently vinyl and preformed aluminum are more common. All slope away from the house. If the drip caps are damaged or missing you might be jeopardizing your new siding job.

1. Adding New Drip Caps. Drip caps are applied after old siding is removed. Cut caps so they overhang the ends of the molding by 1/4 inch. Put the upper flange behind the building paper and nail with 6d galvanized nails every 6 inches.

2. Sealing the Cap. Seal the open ends of the vinyl or aluminum cap with caulk. If you use aluminum drip caps snip the ends after the cap has been installed so that the material wraps the molding.

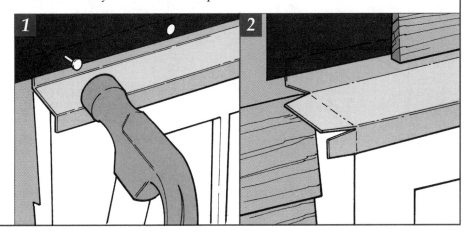

Replacing Windowsills

Windowsills take a beating over the years because of the ravages of sun and moisture. They are not easy to replace, but the job is well worth tackling before residing your house.

1 **Removing Molding.** From inside the house, raise the sash. Then remove the stool (the piece that lays flat on the sill) and the apron (trim beneath the stool).

2 **Removing the Sill.** Use a coarse-cut handsaw to cut through the sill. Use a 1- to 2-inch wood chisel to split and pull out the pieces. Remove nails.

3 **Replacing the Sill.** Cut a replacement sill to fit. Prime the new pieces before installation. Windowsills that are close to ground level (and other places where moisture may be a problem) are also coated with wood preservative.

4 **Nailing the Sill.** Use 16d galvanized finishing nails to install the new sill. Drill pilot holes to avoid splits. Nail from underneath into the side jambs.

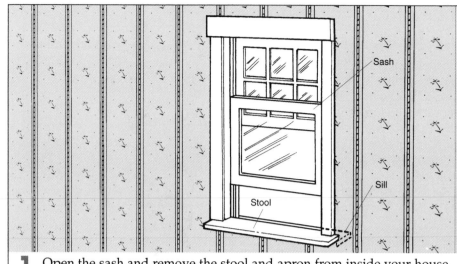

1 Open the sash and remove the stool and apron from inside your house.

2 Cut the old sill in half and remove it by splitting it with a chisel. Pull out all nails.

3 Cut a new sill to fit and slip it into place.

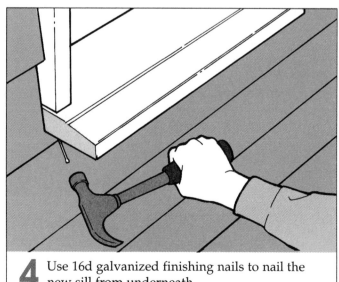

4 Use 16d galvanized finishing nails to nail the new sill from underneath.

SELECTING & INSTALLING WOOD PLANK SIDING

Clapboards and other styles of wood plank siding last for decades, even centuries when correctly installed and maintained. Beautiful and workable, wood plank siding has long been a popular choice among homeowners and the application process is well within the range of do-it-yourselfers.

SIDING TYPE		SIZE	6 INCH AND NARROWER	8 INCH AND WIDER
	Beveled This popular, traditional style is for horizontal applications only. Bungalow (sometimes called Colonial) is slightly thicker then standard. To avoid splitting, do not nail through overlapping pieces.	1×2 1×4 1×6 1×8 1×10 1×12 1¼×6 1¼×8 1¼×10 1¼×12	1-inch overlap recommended. Apply one nail wherever a board crosses a stud. Nail just above the 1-inch overlap.	1-inch overlap recommended. Apply one nail wherever a board crosses a stud. Nail just above the 1-inch overlap.
	Board-on-Board ***Board-and-Batten*** Ideal for vertical applications these boards have smooth, rough, or saw-textured surfaces. Requires horizontal nailing members. Do not nail through overlapping pieces.	1/2×4 1/2×5 1/2×6 5/8×8 5/8×10 3/4×6 3/4×8 3/4×10	1-inch overlap recommended. Apply one nail wherever a board crosses a stud. Nail just above the 1-inch overlap.	1-inch overlap recommended. Apply one nail wherever a board crosses a stud. Nail just above the 1-inch overlap.
	Dolly Varden Thicker than beveled siding and with a rabbeted overlap, this type comes smooth or saw textured. For horizontal applications only. Do not nail through overlapping pieces.	Standard 3/4×6 3/4×8 3/4×10 Thick 1×6 1×8 1×10	Apply one nail wherever a board crosses a stud, just above the 1/2-inch rabbet.	Apply one nail wherever a board crosses a stud, just above the 1/2-inch rabbet. Leave 1/8 inch for expansion.
	Drop Available in a variety of patterns including cupped, beveled, and beaded upper edges, drop siding can be applied vertically or horizontally. Some styles have tongue-and-groove joints, some shiplapped joints. Do not nail through overlapping pieces.	1/2×4 1/2×5 1/2×6 5/8×8 5/8×10 3/4×6 3/4×8 3/4×10	1-inch overlap recommended. Apply one nail wherever a board crosses a stud, just above the 1-inch overlap.	1-inch overlap recommended. Apply one nail wherever a board crosses a stud, just above the 1-inch overlap.
	Tongue and Groove Available in a variety of patterns, this style can be applied vertically or horizontally. Do not nail through overlapping pieces. Tongue widths can vary.	1×4 1×6 1×8 1×10	Use casing nails on tongue-and-groove joints, applying so they will be covered (blind nailed) by overlap.	Face nail with two siding or box nails, 3 to 4 inches apart. Leave 1/8 inch for expansion.

SIDING TYPE	SIZE	6 INCH AND NARROWER	8 INCH AND WIDER
Channel Rustic This style is ideal for horizontal or vertical applications where variable moisture conditions prevail. Ample overlaps allow for movement without altering appearance. Do not nail through overlapping pieces.	3/4×6 3/4×8 3/4×10	Apply one nail wherever a board crosses a stud, 1 inch above the bottom edge.	Face nail with two siding or box nails, 3 to 4 inches apart. Leave 1/8 inch for expansion.
Log Cabin With a rustic style suitable for country or town, this siding is 1½ inch at its thickest dimension. Can be applied horizontally or vertically. Do not nail through overlapping pieces.	1½×6 1½×8 1½×10 1½×12	Apply one nail wherever a nail crosses a stud, 1 inch above the bottom edge.	Face nail with two siding or box nails, 3 to 4 inches apart. Leave 1/8 inch for expansion.

Selecting Siding

Wood siding is made from a wide variety of trees including Douglas fir, larch, and the true firs (ponderosa pine, sugar pine, cedar, and others). Available in many styles, wood siding is both workable and versatile.

Preparing Siding

The installation of wood siding requires planning in advance. Some manufacturer's associations recommend acclimatizing the siding before application. Even though siding is kiln-dried, it may pick up moisture during transit. Lower grades of wood siding retain natural moisture.

Stickering. Separate and stack the siding in a sheltered area away from rain and moisture. Keep the siding at least 3½ inches off the ground and separate the planks with 1×2 or 1×3 furring strips. This process is called "stickering." Acclimate siding for at least a week. The longer, the better.

Prefinishing. For extra protection, prime both sides of the material before applying it. Priming parts that will not be exposed when the siding is installed prolongs the life of the siding. It is easier to apply a coat of primer before installation than it is to prime after installation.

Stickering. Stack the siding as shown and let it acclimatize for a week.

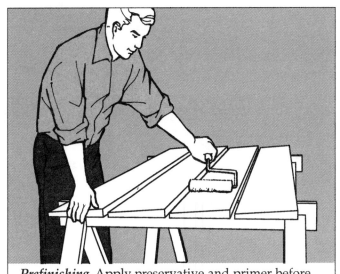

Prefinishing. Apply preservative and primer before the siding is installed rather than after.

Installing Horizontal Siding

Once the trim has been repaired, replaced or removed, and the building paper has been applied, inspect the following areas of the house.

Checking the Foundation. Determine whether your foundation steps down to another level or is on one level around the perimeter of the house. If it steps down, anticipate how to make a smooth transition between courses. Find the lowest corner of the house and work from there.

Choosing a Reference Point. Siding is applied in such a way that it lines up with the bottom edges of windowsills. Determine which set of first-story windows are most visible from the street and make them your reference point. Keep in mind that the level you set for each course will wrap all the way around the house. In some areas it may not ideally align with windows, trim or doors. Make sure awkward alignments occur away from the public side of the house. Decide which second-story windows predominate from the street. Measure the distance from the bottom edge of the windowsills to the bottom edge of the first-story windows below.

Finishing at the Eaves. Avoid ending at the eaves with a thin, unsightly piece of siding. A frieze board and molding not only adds interest and ornament to the house, but also covers awkward gaps. To the extent you can, adjust the overlap of your shingle courses to not only hit windowsills, but finish off the wall gracefully. The story pole helps plan the job (see page 33).

Checking the Foundation. Look for areas where the foundation stair-steps. Plan a smooth transition between courses.

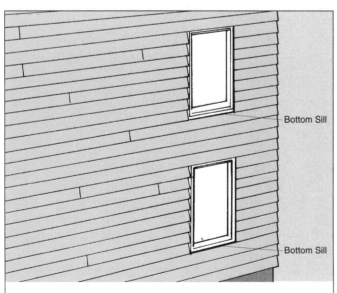

Bottom Sill

Bottom Sill

Choosing a Reference Point. The bottom sills of first- and second-story windows are used as reference points.

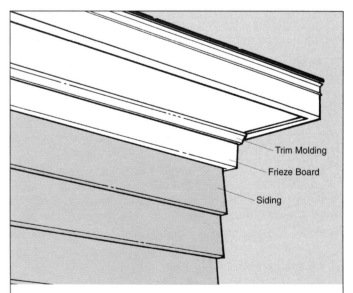

Trim Molding

Frieze Board

Siding

Finishing at the Eaves. Determine the siding overlap at the eaves. A frieze board is sometimes added to finish off the siding.

Choosing the Right Exposure

"Exposure" is the area of siding that is exposed to the weather. It is measured from the lower edge of a piece of siding or shingle to the lower edge of the above course. Carpenters often refer to exposure as the amount of siding "to the weather."

1 Use a piece of 1×4 as a story pole to align the courses of the siding.

As long as courses are adequately overlapped (a minimum of one inch), exposure is a question of aesthetics. Remain true to the style of your house when choosing the exposure.

Making a Story Pole

A story pole is used to predict the layout of siding courses. This prevents unsightly mistakes later. If there is a great deal of variation in sill heights, pick the sides of the house in which appearance is most important and work from there. The goal is to install the siding in such a way that the bottom edge of a course is even with the bottom edge of the windowsills.

1 **Choosing a Length**. Use a piece of 1×4 to create a story pole. If the house is one story the length of the pole will be a few inches longer than the distance from one inch below the top edge of the foundation to the bottom of the fascia or frieze. If the house is two or more stories, make the pole a few inches longer than the distance from the top of the foundation to the bottom of a second-story windowsill.

2 **Setting the Marks.** Measure the distance between the foundation and the first-story windowsill allowing an extra inch where the siding overlaps the top of the foundation. Divide this distance into portions that are as equal as possible to the exposure you have chosen. Mark the story pole in sections equal to the distance between each course. For laying out exposures of odd measurements (such as $4\,^{11}/_{16}$), it is easier to set a compass than to use a measuring tape.

3 **Checking the Courses.** Hold the stick so that one of the marks is even with the bottom of the windowsill. Double-check the point at which the course mark strikes the foundation. If the house has an upper story, use the story pole to check alignment. If necessary, the amount of exposed siding can be adjusted by as much as 1/2 inch without becoming noticeable.

Walk around the house checking the courses and how they will align with windows, doors and trim. Transfer the marks on the pole to the most public corner of the house.

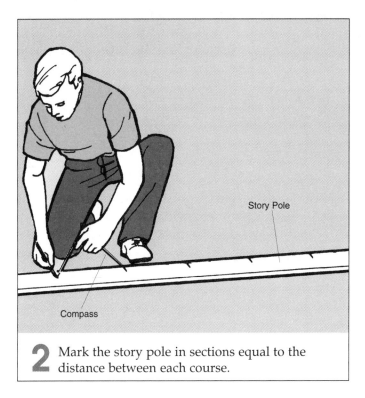

2 Mark the story pole in sections equal to the distance between each course.

3 Check and adjust how the courses will align with the windows, doors, and trim.

Installing the First Course

1 **Installing Starter Strip.** The starter strip is not necessary for siding that has rabbeted or tongue-and-groove joints. It is necessary for siding that uses overlapping boards. Make the starter strip out of stock that is 2 or 3 inches wide and as thick as the siding at the point of course overlap. Nail this strip along the base of the wall just above the foundation.

2 **Getting a Level Start.** Do not assume the foundation is level (particularly if you have an older home). Mark the height of the top of the first siding course at both corners of the wall you are siding. Strike a chalk line and check it with a spirit level. If the line is not level hold a piece of siding against the wall with one end at the low point of the chalk line. Place the level on the top of the board and mark it at the opposite end when level. Strike a new guideline.

3 **Cutting Siding.** Use a circular saw, or better yet, a radial arm saw or power miter saw (with long side benches) to provide a quick, square cut. Use a finish crosscut blade. Measure and cut the first piece so it ends at a wall stud. This is important because a stud provides firm nailing for both sides of the joint. A framing square or angle square helps to quickly lay out a perpendicular cut.

4 **Marking the Next Course.** After installing each piece of siding, mark it with a guideline for the bottom of the next course of siding. You can do this with a chalkline or a pencil and combination square.

5 **Nailing the First Course.** Nail wood carefully. Hammering the nail too far may crack the wood. Nails must penetrate framing members and sheathing by 1½ inches. To prevent nails from splitting the siding, predrill near the ends.

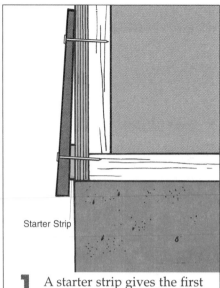

1 A starter strip gives the first course the proper bevel.

2 Strike a line for the top edge and check it for level.

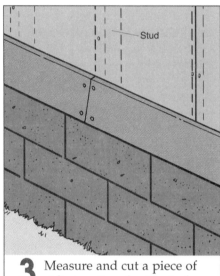

3 Measure and cut a piece of siding so it ends at a stud.

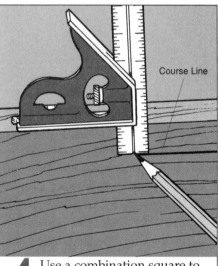

4 Use a combination square to mark course lines.

5 Nail the first course 1 in. from the top edge and 1½ in. from the bottom edge.

Choosing the Right Nail

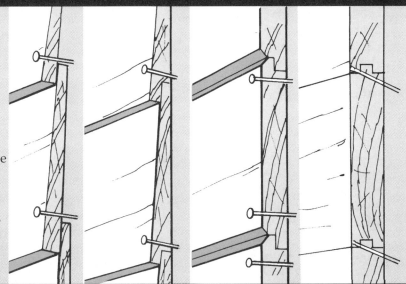

Different types of horizontal siding are nailed differently. Shown, from left, are nailing patterns for clapboard, rabbeted, shiplap, and tongue-and groove siding.

Use ring, spiral-shanked, or hot-dipped galvanized shanks to prevent nails from loosening with time. Although expensive, stainless steel nails do not rust or corrode. Aluminum nails are less expensive, but corrode when they come in contact with galvanized (zinc-coated) metal. In addition, they bend very easily. Galvanized nails are the least expensive type of nail. They cannot be used on cedar siding that has a clear finish because their nailheads tend to discolor. Blunt or diamond pointed nails are most commonly used and also help reduce splitting.

Working Up the Wall

1 Getting the Right Length. Cut the siding to length. Be careful that the joint is centered on a stud.

Note: Joints that are not nailed to the framing are very likely to loosen later. Do not nail into the sheathing alone.

2 Aligning the Course Line. Tack a nail into the course guideline where one end of the siding will be nailed. Rest one end of the siding on this nail. (A helper can hold it for you but a tacked nail is more reliable and quicker).

3 Nailing the Siding. Position nails just above the overlap for beveled siding; just above the rabbet for Dolly Varden siding, and 1 inch from the bottom for drop siding and log cabin profiles. Blind-nail tongue-and-groove siding diagonally through the tongue. Blind nailing means the nails won't be seen after the groove of the next board covers the tongue.

At the opposite end of the siding board, begin nailing at the second stud from the end. Double-check alignment on the course line before hammering the nail home. Check the opposite end and nail it at least

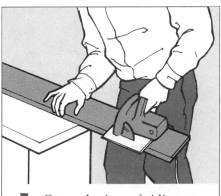

1 Cut each piece of siding so that both ends hit a stud.

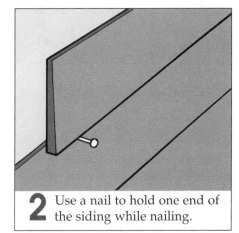

2 Use a nail to hold one end of the siding while nailing.

Course Line

3 Check alignment against the course line before nailing.

4 To avoid splitting the wood drill a pilot hole for each nail.

one stud in from the end. Remove the tack and complete the nailing.

4 Nailing the Joints. When adding the adjacent piece, nail the joints last. Be sure to predrill them

to avoid splitting. Add three or four additional courses being careful to stagger joints so that no joint is directly over another. At every fourth or fifth course check with a spirit level and make adjustments accordingly.

Selecting & Installing Wood Plank Siding **35**

Siding Around Windows

1 Drilling the Ends. Siding simply butts up against window trim. Drill pilot holes before nailing near the ends of siding pieces.

2 Marking the Notch. Despite efforts to plan around the possibility, the siding above some windows must be notched. Tack a nail into the guideline, slide the piece in place and mark the height of the notch. Then mark the width of the notch while holding the board over the window.

3 Cutting the Notch. After marking the board use a combination circular saw blade to make a plunge cut. Set the blade 1/8 inch deeper than the cut. Make the two crosscuts and finish them with a handsaw. If the drip cap is wood, you may have to bevel the notch with a utility knife or block plane.

4 Installing the Piece. Install the piece above the window. Nail it along the top every 16 inches. Caulk around the window.

Siding at Gables

1 Capturing the Angle. Use a sliding T-bevel to capture the angle of the cut for transfer to the new piece of siding. Align the body of the tool with the bottom edge of a clapboard and adjust the blade to run along the slope of the rake. As an alternative, make a template of the angle using scrap held against the underside of the rake.

1 Butt siding up against window trim. Caulk the seams.

2 Siding around some windows must be notched to fit.

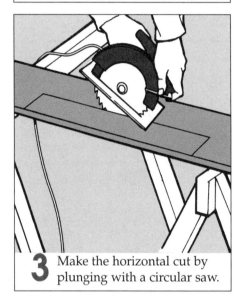

3 Make the horizontal cut by plunging with a circular saw.

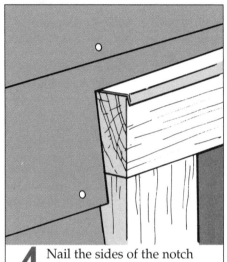

4 Nail the sides of the notch and every 16 in. along the top.

Scrap Pieces

1 There are two ways to capture the angle at gables: Use a T-bevel or use scraps of siding to transfer the angle.

2 Locating the Angle. Locate the angle by measuring along the course guideline and cut accordingly. Save the scrap as a marking guide for other pieces.

3 Drilling Pilot Holes. To avoid splits, drill pilot holes for nails nearest the rake. Caulk the joint between the siding and the trim.

Angle Marking Guide

2 Measure along the course guideline and cut accordingly.

3 Drill pilot holes near the rake before nailing.

Corner Treatments

Corners impact upon the appearance of a house and, depending on the type used, affect the difficulty of the job.

Metal Corners. When it comes to beveled siding, metal corner caps allow for error and are an easy and neat finish. Do not wrap them too tightly around the corner. These also can be opened up for application around the corners of bay and bow windows.

Overlapping Trim. For flat siding with no indentations, apply trim over the siding. Nail with 8d gal-vanized nails side by side, at 16-inch intervals.

Butting Trim. Clapboards do not create a flat surface, so it is not advisable to overlap the trim. Install the trim before clapboards are installed, compensating for walls that are not plumb. Siding is cut to meet the trim squarely with a butt joint. The outside edge follows the house, while the inside edge is attached plumb. Use 8d galvanized nails every 16 inches.

Mitered. Creating mitered corners requires skill and a circular saw, chop box or radial arm saw. A 6d galvanized nail joins the two edges of the siding. Drill a pilot hole before nailing them together.

Inside Corner Strip. Used in a corner so siding can be butted against it on both sides. Nail in place with 8d galvanized nails every 16 inches.

Overlapping Corner Strip. This quick approach covers irregularities in siding gaps at the inside corner. Nail it in place with 8d galvanized nails every 16 inches.

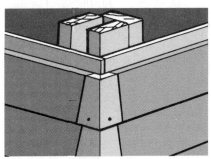

Metal Corners

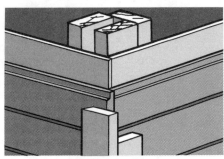

Overlapping Trim

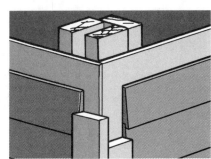

Butting Trim

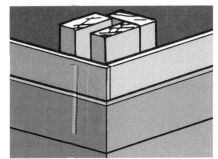

Mitered

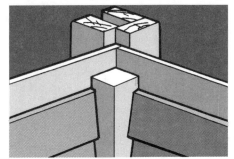

Inside Corner Strip

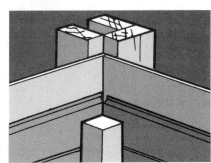

Overlapping Corner Strip

Furring Strip

1 If the sheathing is not solid wood or plywood, furring strips must be attached.

Applying Vertical Plank Siding

Vertical siding is installed very much like horizontal siding with one important exception: Vertical siding can only be fastened directly to wood sheathing that is at least 5/8 inch thick. For thinner wood sheathing, or for fiberboard, furring strips must be used. Because many newer homes are sheathed with fiberboard or 1/2-inch plywood, furring is often needed.

1 Adding Furring strips. Add 1x3 or 1x4 nailers 16 inches on center horizontally. Make sure that nails penetrate sheathing and framing 1 1/2 inches. Use cement-coated common nails of a sufficient length (8d nails typically work).

2 Starting Plumb. Never trust the corner of the house to be a plumb starting point. Choose a point that is one plank width away from a corner. With a plumb bob or a spirit level held beside a piece of siding, mark at upper and lower ends and strike a chalk line. Check for plumb every sixth board or so. If the boards get far off of plumb, compensate by making minor adjustments in spacing on the next two or three boards.

3 Making Horizontal Joints. Always use full lengths of boards and avoid horizontal joints when possible. Joints must fall over furring strips. Bevel the ends of abutting joints so that water that penetrates drains away from the house.

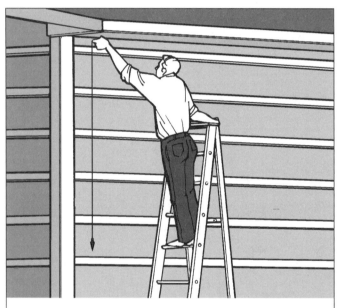

2 Use a plumb bob or level held against a plank to establish a plumb beginning point. Check for plumb every sixth board or so.

3 Bevel horizontal joints so penetrating water drains away from the house.

Plywood Horizontal Siding

Plywood lap siding is less expensive than solid wood siding and resists splitting when nailed. Plywood is relatively easy to handle. Although it is heavier than wood siding, it is lighter and more rigid than hardboard. If you are using 1/2-inch or thicker plywood sheathing, vertical joints need not be over wall studs. Start plywood siding no less than 6 inches above grade.

Plywood is installed much like wood horizontal siding, except that special care must be taken to keep moisture from penetrating vertical joints and the edges. Leave a 1/16- to 1/8-inch gap in places where the siding meets trim. Caulk the gap with a non-hardening caulk.

Beveled Edge

4 For trim that does not overlap, bevel the edge for a neat fit.

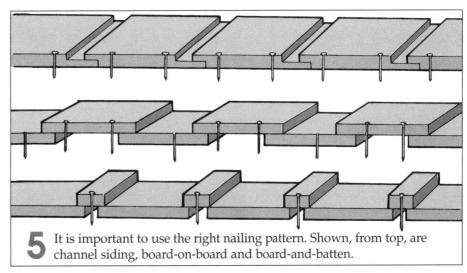

5 It is important to use the right nailing pattern. Shown, from top, are channel siding, board-on-board and board-and-batten.

4 **Making Neat Joints.** In places where the trim does not overlap the siding, use a block plain to bevel the siding where it meets the trim.

5 **Nailing Right.** Different types of nails are used depending upon the type of siding installed (see page 35). Avoid nailing through two pieces of vertical siding. Fasten pieces independently in the manner shown.

Hardboard Horizontal Siding

Hardboard siding is among the simplest forms of plank siding to install. Two systems are available, both of which are self-aligning. A newer sys-

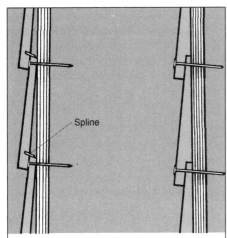

Hardboard Horizontal Siding. Hardboard siding either uses splines and allows blind nailing or is rabbeted along the bottom edge.

tem has horizontal splines that hook over the course below and permit blind nailing. This system is prepainted with color-coordinated accessories such as inside and outside corners, caulk and trim. The other hardboard siding system has rabbeted joints that hook over the course below and cannot be blind nailed. The instructions below are for the system that uses splines. Rabbeted hardboard planks are installed exactly the same way that natural wood siding is installed. (See page 32).

Hardboard is heavy, but it is an affordable, long-lasting siding alternative. One decided benefit is that hardboard splits only if nailed extremely close to the edge. Hardboard siding systems are ideal for do-it-yourselfers who want to transform their home quickly.

Caution: Moisture is the enemy of unsealed hardboard. It is wise to seal all vertical edges with caulk immediately after installation. Take care to avoid cracking the surface when nailing. Spot prime and touch up damage done to the surface. Do not allow installed hardboard to touch masonry.

Applying Hardboard Siding

Hardboard siding is installed similarly to other types of horizontal siding. Check for level every six courses or so and locate vertical joints over wall

studs. Hardboard siding must be fastened to framing members that are no more than 16 inches apart. Leave 3/16-inch gaps at all vertical junctures, and seal every joint as soon as possible.

1 **Installing Starter Strip.** Make sure that the first course is no closer than 6 inches to the ground when installed. Install the metal starter strip along the bottom edge of the sheathing or furring. Level it and then nail every 12 inches with 6d galvanized box nails.

When residing with hardboard, remove old siding or apply furring strips at wall studs. If siding over masonry, add a vapor barrier over the masonry and then use furring that is at least 1½ inches deep.

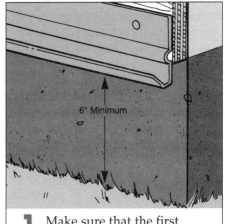

6" Minimum

1 Make sure that the first course is no closer than 6 in. to the ground.

2 Installing Inside Corners. If the job has inside corners, cut and nail a metal inside corner in place. Use 6d galvanized box nails at 12-inch intervals. A primed piece of 1⅛- × 1⅛-inch wood also can be used.

3 Adding the First Course. Measure and cut the first piece of siding so that it ends at a wall stud. Cut the siding face up with a fine-toothed handsaw or face down with a circular saw equipped with a combination blade. Set the first piece of siding in place so that the plastic spline on the back locks into the metal starter strip. Hold the siding down firmly and nail at each wall stud 5/8 inch down from the top edge of the siding. Use galvanized box nails that penetrate 1½ inches into the wall stud. Use factory-finished, color-matched nails in places

where the nailheads are visible (for instance, at inside corners and butt joints). Power nailers are available for installing this type of siding. Nail from one end to the other. Do not nail toward the center from both ends. Do not nail at the location of a butt joint until the joint molding is in place.

4 Fastening Butt Joints. Push the joint molding onto the end of the piece of siding that is already installed. Leave a 3/16-inch expansion gap at the joint. Slide the next piece of siding into the joint. Nail 5/8 inch down from the top edge of the siding, on both sides of the joint. Make sure the nails hit the wall stud. Use a spirit level to check for level every four to six courses. If the siding is off by a substantial amount make slight adjustments on two or three courses until they get back on track.

5 Siding Around Windows and Doors. Because the manufactured spline does not let you vary the amount of siding face exposed to the weather, the tops and bottoms of windows will have to be notched. Maintain a 3/16-inch gap around windows and doors; it will be caulked later. Make sure that drip caps over windows and doors are in good condition.

6 Spacing over Roofs. Check that flashing is in good condition at junctions between walls and roofing. Maintain at least a 2-inch gap between the bottom edge of the siding and the roofing surface.

7 Finishing Outside Corners. Finish outside corners with aluminum corners, often available prepainted to match the siding.

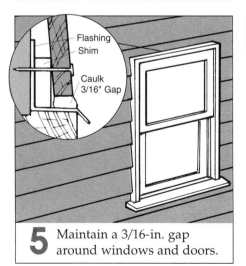

2 Use 6d galvanized box nails to install inside metal corners.

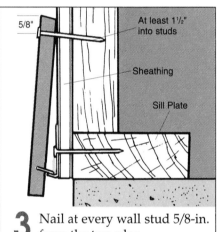

5/8"
At least 1½" into studs
Sheathing
Sill Plate

3 Nail at every wall stud 5/8-in. from the top edge.

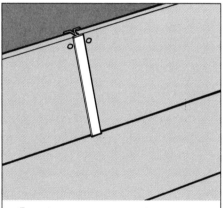

4 Use joint molding for a consistent 3/16-in. gap at butt joints.

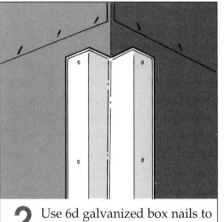

Flashing
Shim
Caulk 3/16" Gap

5 Maintain a 3/16-in. gap around windows and doors.

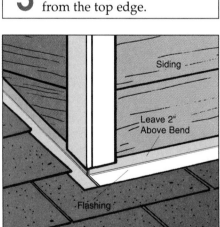

Siding
Leave 2" Above Bend
Flashing

6 Do not install siding closer than 2 in. from roofing.

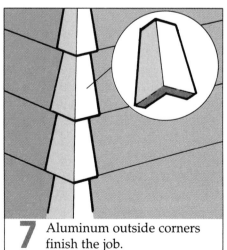

7 Aluminum outside corners finish the job.

SELECTING & INSTALLING PANEL SIDING

Panel siding is a good choice if you want to cover the house quickly and inexpensively. At a small cost per square foot, panels gobble up large chunks of territory in a single application. Do not, however, let the ease of application seduce you into relaxing on the details. Plywood and hardboard are more vulnerable to the elements than other siding options and must be sealed well.

Plywood Panel Siding

Plywood siding, like all plywood, is composed of an odd number of wood veneer layers that are cross-laminated. In other words, the grain of each veneer runs across the grain of the veneers glued to each side of it. Cross-lamination gives plywood siding some advantages over solid wood siding. For one, the siding is very strong in all directions. Humidity changes cause solid wood to expand and contract across the grain. Cross-lamination in plywood cancels out most of this tendency, making plywood siding more stable than solid wood. Finally, while solid wood tends to split when nailed close to the ends, it virtually is impossible to split plywood by nailing.

One disadvantage to using plywood is its tendency to delaminate. If moisture gets between the plies, they may come apart. This happens when the plywood edge—its most vulnerable point—is not adequately covered, or when a crack or hole in the surface of the plywood allows moisture to enter. To avoid delamination, apply trim pieces properly and caulk and seal the siding.

Plywood siding is available with a variety of veneer surfaces: Douglas fir and southern pine are less expensive options; Western red cedar and redwood are used for the more premium exterior grades. Surface treatments for plywood range from V-groove, channel groove, deep groove, brushed and rough sawn, to medium-density overlaid (MDO) plywood that is faced with a resin-fiber sheet and available in a variety of textures. Some newer types of plywood have a final layer of pigmented hardboard that is textured similarly to wood or stucco.

Common thicknesses for plywood siding are 1 1/32-, 3/8-, 7/16-, 15/32-, 1/2-, 19/32-, 5/8- and 3/4-inch. (Plywood panels suitable for soffits and exterior utility uses, range from 1/4- to 3/4-inches in thickness.)

Choosing Plywood. Every sheet of plywood carries a stamp that designates the composition and intended use of the panel. The two capital letters, such as A-C or B-C, indicate the grade of veneer used on both faces of the plywood. "A" is the best; "D" is the worst. The span rating (for example, 24 on-center or 16 on-center) indicates the maximum distance the siding can tolerate between framing members. Perhaps the most important information on the stamp indicates the type of glue used. Use panels that have the EXTERIOR designation.

Caution: *"Exposure 1" or "Exposure 2" ratings do not mean that the material is suitable for siding. These numbers merely indicate that the material can be exposed to the elements for a limited period during construction.*

Most local lumberyards have what is variously called T 1-11 (short for Textured 1-11) or O.C. siding. This type of siding has grooves that run the length of the sheet at 4-, 8- or 12-inch intervals or at random distances. Grooves may be channeled with a fluted appearance; kerfed with a narrow flat channel; reverse board-and-batten with wider flat grooves, or V-shaped. The face of the siding is available in a variety of textures including relief-grained (an exaggerated look of natural wood grain), rough-sawn and smooth.

Plywood siding is available in standard 4×8-foot sheets, and also in 9- and 10-foot lengths. If longer sheets would make the job easier and neater, it is well worth shopping around to find them.

Plywood Panel Siding. Veneers with alternating grain direction make plywood strong.

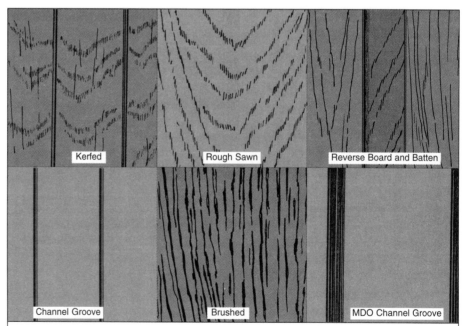

Kerfed — Rough Sawn — Reverse Board and Batten — Channel Groove — Brushed — MDO Channel Groove

Choosing Plywood. Plywood panels come in a variety of textures and styles (depending on how the veneer is sawn, grooved, brushed or surfaced). Ratings stamped on plywood provide valuable information.

Preparing the Walls. Building paper or felt around windows safeguard against weather penetration.

1 Prime the edges of plywood if they are not prepainted or hardboard surfaced.

2 Furring strips may be necessary if walls have serious dents or voids.

Preparing the Walls

Plywood siding panels that are 5/8 inches thick or thicker can be nailed directly to studs. Thinner plywood panels require a smooth, flat wall surface. Use a thicker plywood to straighten out irregularities and to cover rough existing siding.

Building paper usually is not required for plywood (check your local codes), but you may want to apply it as extra protection around windows, doors and plywood sheets.

1 **Priming Ends.** Panels are vulnerable to damage caused by water. Before installing siding panels, apply a primer or first coat of stain on all butt edges. These areas are impossible to reach after installation.

2 **Handling Gaps and Indentations.** If the surface is very irregular, use furring strips (1×2, 1×3 or 1×4 pieces) attached vertically every 16 or 24 inches (depending on the material).

3 **Adding the Trim.** At this time apply the trim that butts against the siding. Ornamental trim bands above the foundation are applied before panels, while outside corner trim, many types of inside corner trim, and trim along the eaves are applied after siding panels (see page 47).

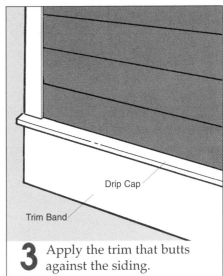

3 Apply the trim that butts against the siding.

Installing Plywood Panels

Plywood siding panels are heavy and awkward to handle. Because of their size, it is difficult for a person who is working alone to see whether or not they fit correctly all around. You'll need someone to hold the panel in place so you can step back to view the fit.

1 Getting Started. The first panel must be positioned correctly. If it is out of plumb, all subsequent panels are affected. If the panels have gotten out of plumb as you work, correct them gradually. For example, make a 1/8-inch correction in three succeeding panels rather than a 3/8-inch correction at one panel. Position the first panel so its vertical joint is over a wall stud.

Cut the panel reverse side up. The splintering caused by a circular saw is not visible that way. If you must cut the panels face up, minimize splintering by first scoring the line with a utility knife.

Plywood and hardboard siding ideally extend at least 1 inch below the sheathing. More importantly, it must be kept clearly off the ground and out of standing water. Prepare for the worst weather conditions. Wherever possible use full sheets rather than cobbling together small pieces. (Paint will not camouflage the joints.)

2 Leaving Gaps. Do not assume "the tighter, the better." Panel siding expands and contracts with weather, as do the materials it butts up against. It is best to provide slight gaps in the places materials meet. Specifications often call for 1/16 inch between shiplapped panels, 1/8 inch between straight-edge panels and 1/8 inch in places where panels come up against other building materials. Use an 8d nail diameter as a guide. In practice, of course, no one is able to maintain these gaps accurately everywhere (especially residing jobs because the cuts often are not square). Maintain small gaps in most places. If you have to use a hammer

1 Tack the first sheet in place, and check for plumb.

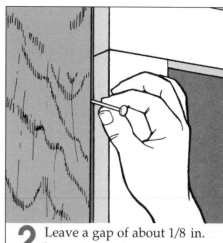

2 Leave a gap of about 1/8 in. between butt joints.

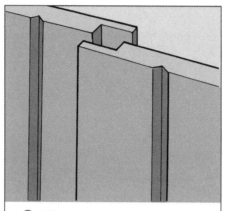

3 The overlapping piece goes on last at every joint.

4 Nail panels 6 in. around the edge and 12 in. in the middle.

to force a piece into position, it is too tight.

3 Nailing at Overlaps. When using a shiplap joint (probably the most common for plywood siding) the overlapping piece goes on last at each joint. To preserve a tight seal leave the right-hand edge nail-free until you have overlapped it with the next panel. Nail through both sides of the shiplap at once.

4 Nailing Panels. Use nonstaining box, casing or siding nails that penetrate the studs 1½ inches. Place the nails at 6-inch intervals around the perimeter and 12-inch intervals elsewhere. The job is simple if you are covering wood sheathing or siding that holds a nail well. If not, plan the job so that joints meet in the center of studs.

Z-bar

5 Install Z-bar before a second course of plywood panels.

5 Installing Second Courses. When joining two panels vertically use 6d galvanized nails at 12-inch intervals to install a piece of Z-bar on top of the lower panel. (Z-bar is made of painted aluminum or galvanized sheet metal and is available in 10-foot lengths.) Then install the panel above it.

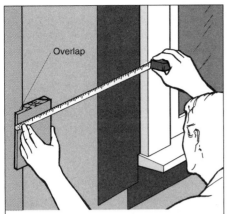

1 Position the scrap at the panel edge and measure from the extent of its overlap.

Siding Scrap

2 Allow for the thickness of the siding when measuring under a windowsill.

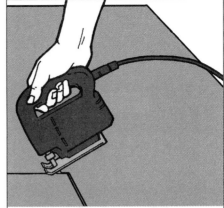

3 Support the panel on sawhorses and use a saber saw to make the cutout.

4 Hook the lower edge of the cutout under the sill and rest the top edge on the brickmold.

Cutting Around Windows & Doors

1 **Choosing a Reference Point.** When possible, use the leading edge of the previous sheet as a guide for cutouts (such as with windows and doors). If you are using shiplap plywood, be sure to note the overlap of the joint when measuring. Use a piece of scrap that includes the overlap portion of the joint to help measure. Position the scrap at the panel edge and measure from the overlap.

2 **Measuring the Cut.** Measure from the top of the sheet to the top of the opening. Measure from the bottom of the sheet to the bottom of the windowsill. When measuring beneath the sill, use a scrap of siding

to indicate where the siding will touch the inclined sill. Use a straightedge or chalkline to make precise lines.

3 **Making the Cut.** Use a saber saw to cut out the waste area.

4 **Installing the Piece.** Due to the incline of the windowsill, the piece must be slid into place. Hook the bottom of the cutout beneath the sill. Set the top over the brick mold of the window and slide the panel in place. Maintain a 1/8-inch gap around the window.

Cutting for Gable Ends

Fitting panels under a gable always involves one course of panels on top of another course of panels. The

Z-bar

1 Z-bar flashing is installed on stacked siding panels.

course below provides a base line for installing the course under the gable. Still, measuring the angled cuts correctly and hefting the panels into place safely, means this is a two-person job.

1 **Installing Flashing.** Z-bar flashing is installed wherever siding panels are stacked on top of each other. Nail it every 12 inches using 6d galvanized nails. Add drip caps above windows within the gable when butting to existing molding above a door or window.

2 **Measuring the Incline.** Plan the job so that joints between second course panels do not line up with the joints of the first course. Channels or grooves must line up.

2 Chalk a plumb line under the gable to mark panel height.

3 Measure chalk line. Allow 1/8 in. for expansion.

4 Cut from the back of the panel to minimize splintering.

Measure the length of the base of the panel. Then use a chalkline to strike a plumb line indicating the necessary height of the panel.

3 Measuring for Height. Measure the length of the chalk line less 1/8 inch (for an expansion gap). This measurement equals the height of the triangular piece of siding needed.

4 Cutting the Panel. Lay out these measurements on the back of a panel. Draw or chalk a straight line between them. Cut with a circular saw equipped with a plywood blade. Set the blade no more than 1/4 inch deeper than the thickness of the plywood.

Cutting Round Holes

Round holes, such as those needed for an outdoor faucet, require special cuts.

1. Measuring to the Center. Using the edge of the last installed panel as a reference point, measure to the center of the pipe. Measure from the top of the pipe to the bottom of the last installed panel. Transfer these measurements to the next panel to be installed.

2. Cutting the Hole. Drill a hole using a drill bit or hole saw that is 1/4 inch larger than the pipe.

3. Cutting Access. To allow the panel to slip into place, cut out a strip the same width as the hole to the nearest edge of the panel (or the least obvious edge). Save the cutout.

4. Replacing the Strip. After installing the panel, nail or glue the strip in place. Caulk the strip well. If the strip is under the faucet it is especially susceptible to water damage.

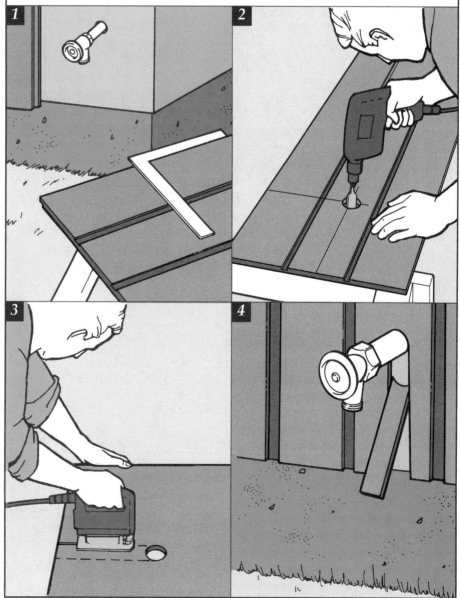

Making Beveled Joints

Beveled joints help avoid unsightly gaps at the end joints and create a protective seal against the weather. It takes a bit of practice to cut a beveled joint, but it is worth the effort.

1 **Setting the Saw.** Locate the joint in a place where firm nailing is ensured. Measure the length of the first piece of trim and mark the cut line on the back of the board. Unplug your circular saw and set the blade at a 45-degree angle, but do not trust the setting gauge on the saw; double-check it with an angle square. Using the square as a guide, cut the board and nail it in place as you would any piece of trim. Stop short of nailing at the beveled joint.

2 **Measuring the Second Piece.** Measure the second piece of trim allowing for the overlap of the beveled joint. Mark and cut the board.

3 **Nailing the Joint.** Overlap the beveled joint and install the trim. Drill pilot holes before nailing the joint. Drill at an angle so the nails slant toward the joint.

Trim Options

Choose trim to suit your style. Commonly 1×4 pieces are used. Nail them with 6d or 8d galvanized box nails. Choose either a smooth- or rough-faced wood to complement the siding. If you are using stain, use the same wood for trim and siding.

Apply caulk where siding meets a different material (for instance a window, door or gable rafter).

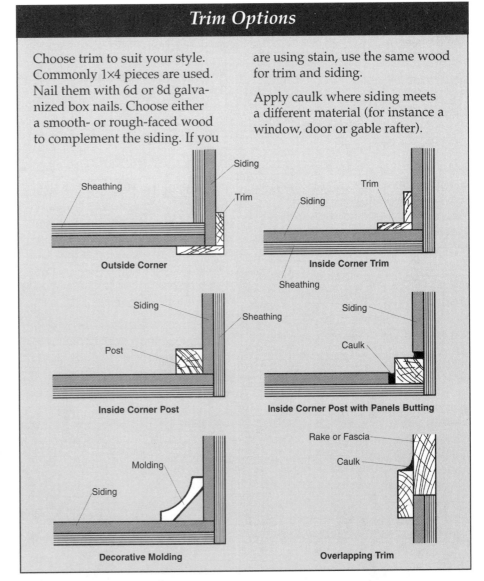

Outside Corner

Inside Corner Trim

Inside Corner Post

Inside Corner Post with Panels Butting

Decorative Molding

Overlapping Trim

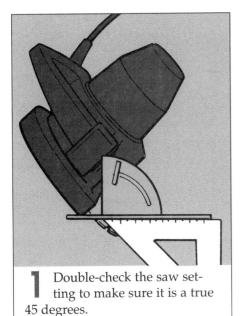

1 Double-check the saw setting to make sure it is a true 45 degrees.

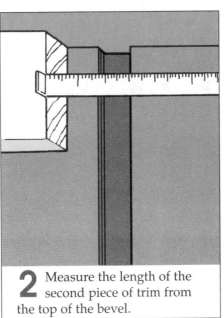

2 Measure the length of the second piece of trim from the top of the bevel.

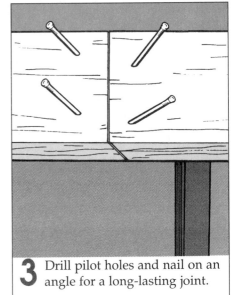

3 Drill pilot holes and nail on an angle for a long-lasting joint.

Hardboard Panel Siding

Hardboard (also called Masonite) is composed of wood that has been reduced to a pulp and then pressed together with heat. It is more dense than natural wood and resists dents. It has no knots or grain.

Hardboard siding must be carefully protected from the weather. When moisture penetrates hardboard, it swells and loses strength. Hardboard pieces that become moist cannot be repaired and must be replaced.

Hardboard siding is available in a variety of textures including weathered wood grain and stucco. Like plywood it is available in panels 4 feet wide, and 8, 9, or 10 feet long.

The application for hardboard siding is similar to that of plywood with the addition of these important steps:

1 **Preparing the Walls.** Mark the stud locations on the foundation, then cover the walls with building wrap or felt. If the walls are covered with waterproof sheathing, no wrap or felt is needed.

2 **Nailing Hardboard.** Because hardboard is heavy, the supporting nails must penetrate at least 1½ inches into wall studs. Use 8d nails. Some manufacturers sell pre-painted, corrosion-resistant nails to match colored panels. Choose these or galvanized box nails.

Nail from top to bottom along the left edge at first, then work horizontally.

Place nails 3/8 inch from the edge at 6-inch intervals. When nailing within the field of the hardboard, space nails at 12-inch intervals.

3 **Nailing Through Shiplap.** To preserve a tight seal, don't nail the right-hand edge until it is overlapped by the next panel. Nail through both sides of the shiplap at once.

4 **Caulking Joints.** Plywood panels are vulnerable to water damage caused by seepage at the edges, so be sure to caulk the 1/8-inch gaps at the end of each day they are installed. Shiplap joints do not have to be caulked.

1 Unlike plywood, hardboard must have building wrap.

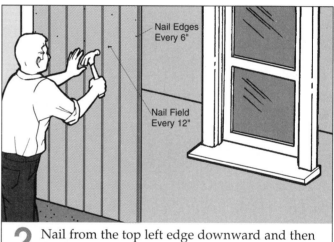

Nail Edges Every 6"

Nail Field Every 12"

2 Nail from the top left edge downward and then across at the intervals shown.

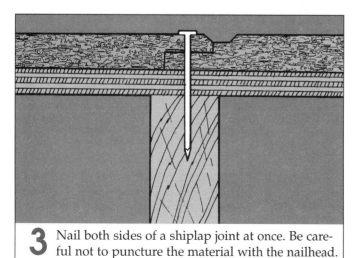

3 Nail both sides of a shiplap joint at once. Be careful not to puncture the material with the nailhead.

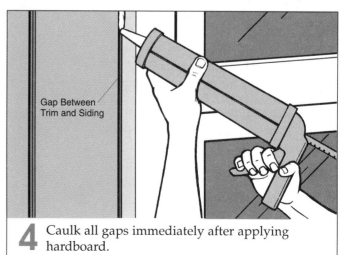

Gap Between Trim and Siding

4 Caulk all gaps immediately after applying hardboard.

SELECTING & INSTALLING WOOD SHINGLES & SHAKES

Wood shingles and shakes possess a beautiful rustic quality that appeals to many homeowners. The act of installing them is labor-intensive, so it really does pay to do it yourself. Shingles and shakes are good materials to work with because the wood is easy to shape and the final results are dramatic.

Choosing Wood Shingles & Shakes

Wood shingles and shakes usually are made of Western red cedar, a long-lasting straight-grained wood. The grain is what gives the wood surprising strength even when it is cut thin. After years of weathering, wood does a much better job of shedding water than might be expected. In addition, wood shingles and shakes have some insulating value and are easily repaired. With correct application and maintenance, they can last for decades.

Choosing Between Shingles & Shakes

Shingles are thinner than shakes and are sawn smooth on both sides. Shakes often are split by hand rather than cut and have a very irregular surface. They are thicker and therefore more durable than shingles.

Straight-split shakes do not taper in thickness (as do all other wood shingles and shakes) and are not intended for residential use.

Both shakes and shingles are available in #1, 2 and 3 grades. Grade #1 is cut from heartwood, a clear (knot-free), completely edge-grained wood that is more resistant to rot than the other grades. It is also the most expensive of the grades. Buy the best grade you can afford.

Grade #2 can contain a limited amount of sapwood which is less rot resistant than heartwood. Grade #2 has some knots and is flat grained. It is acceptable for residential roofing. Use grade #3 shingles or shakes for outbuildings only. Undercoursing is done with #4 shingles.

The shingle length needed is determined by the desired exposure (the length of shingle exposed to weather). Exposure is determined by pitch. Shingle widths vary from 3 to 9 inches.

Shingle & Shake Grades

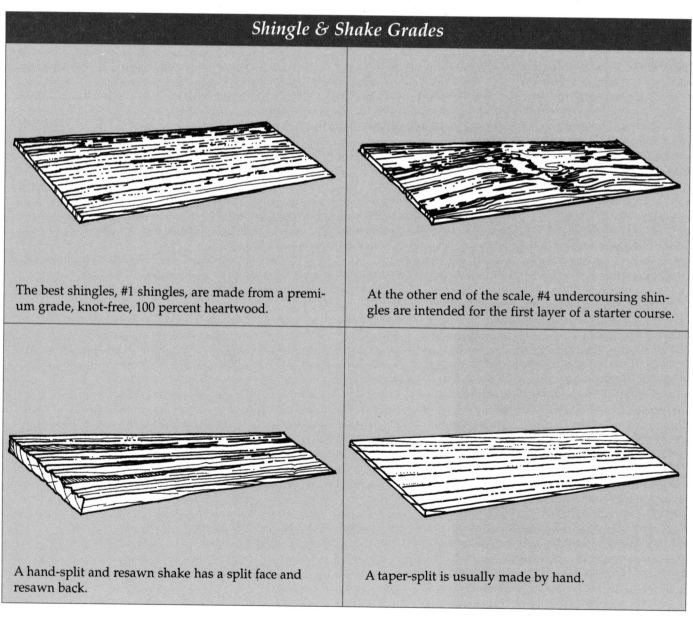

The best shingles, #1 shingles, are made from a premium grade, knot-free, 100 percent heartwood.

At the other end of the scale, #4 undercoursing shingles are intended for the first layer of a starter course.

A hand-split and resawn shake has a split face and resawn back.

A taper-split is usually made by hand.

Estimating Materials

There are many factors that determine how much material is needed: the type of shingle or shake used; whether they will be applied in single or double courses (see page 52), and the amount of exposure desired. After determining the total square footage to be covered, follow these steps to accurately estimate materials.

Choosing an Exposure. Experiment with the amount of exposure you think will look best, but keep in mind that exposure allowances differ depending upon the shingle. Double courses (two layers of shingles for each course) permit greater exposure because the dual layer better keeps out the weather.

Estimating the Shingles. Equipped with your shingle pattern, square footage and exposure, visit a supplier. By consulting charts that factor in shingle type as well as the above variables, an estimate can be made. For typical exposures, four bundles of shingles, or five bundles of shakes, per 100 square feet is sufficient.

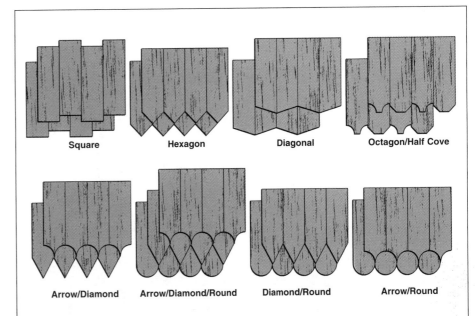

Square   Hexagon   Diagonal   Octagon/Half Cove

Arrow/Diamond   Arrow/Diamond/Round   Diamond/Round   Arrow/Round

Decorative Shingles. Shingle manufacturers have responded to the renewed interest in ornamental shingles by offering a wide range of styles. Typically 5 inches wide and 16 to 18 inches long, shingles are purchased in cartons of 96 pieces (enough to cover 25 square feet at 7½ inch exposure). They can be combined with other shingles, lap siding or board-and-batten application.

Maximum Exposure Guidelines

	Length	Single Course	Double Course
Shingles	16-inch	7½ inches	12 inches
	18-inch	8½ inches	14 inches
	24-inch	11½ inches	16 inches
Resawn Shakes	18-inch	8½ inches	14 inches
	24-inch	11½ inches	18 inches
Taper-Split Shakes	24-inch	11½ inches	18 inches
Straight-Split Shakes	18-inch	8½ inches	14 inches
	24-inch	11½ inches	18 inches

Area Covered by One Square of Shingles

Length	Exposure												
	3½"	4"	4½"	5"	5½"	6"	6½"	7"	7½"	8"	8½"	9"	9½"
16-inch	70	80	90	100	110	120	130	140	150	160	170	180	190
18-inch	—	72½	81½	90½	100	109	118	127	136	145½	154½	163½	172½
24-inch	—	—	—	—	73½	80	86½	93	100	106½	113	120	126½

Length	Exposure												
	10"	10½"	11"	11½"	12"	12½"	13"	13½"	14"	14½"	15"	15½"	16"
16-inch	200	210	220	230	240	—	—	—	—	—	—	—	—
18-inch	181½	191	200	209	218	227	236	245½	254½	—	—	—	—
24-inch	133	140	146½	153	160	166½	173	180	186½	193	200	206½	213

Applying Single-Course Shingles

Shingles are considered a versatile material because course exposure is adjusted so easily. Shingles are applied to new walls or those that have been stripped and covered with building paper or felt. They also are applied directly to beveled siding, and with the help of horizontal furring strips, they may be applied to brick or stucco as well.

1 Planning the Courses. Use a story pole to help establish the starter course (see page 33). Determine the place in which the butt line (bottom edge) of courses intersects the tops and sills of windows. Also, make sure there will be a 4-inch (or greater) course of shingles beneath the eaves. The first course must overlap the foundation by at least 1 inch. Strike a chalk line on the foundation or on the wall above if the foundation is too rough to hold a line.

2 Installing the Starter Course. Install one row of shingles with a gap of 1/8 to 1/4 inch between each shingle to allow for expansion. Use galvanized roofing nails 1 inch above the butt line.

3 Installing a Second Layer. Add a second layer to the starter course. Overlap each joint by at least 1½ inches.

4 Adding the Second Course. Tack a 1x4 along the second layer of the starter course to act as a guide for the bottom of the second course. When installing the shingles, be sure to position nails so that the course above will overlap them by about 1 inch. Hammer two nails into each shingle about 3/4 inch from each edge. For shingles that are wider than 8 inches, add two nails an inch apart in the center. Check every third or fourth course to see that it is level.

1 Use a story pole to set the distance between courses.

2 Use galvanized roofing nails for starter course.

3 Nail a second layer of shingles over the first layer.

4 Overlap first course joints with second course.

5 Allow for expansion around window and door openings.

6 Fasten partial shingles under the eaves with finishing nails.

5 Fitting Windows & Doors. Shingles fitted around windows and doors must have an expansion gap. Hold the shingle in place allowing for the gap and mark it 1/8 to 1/4 inch short of the window molding. Then cut it with a roofing hatchet, a utility knife or a table saw. Smooth the edge with a block plane if needed.

6 Finishing at the Eaves. When setting the exposure for each course of shingles keep in mind that there must be at least 4 inches for the final course at the eaves. If possible, cut several shingles at once on a table saw, radial arm saw or chop box. Nail them in place with galvanized finishing nails.

Shingles can be installed over walls such as beveled siding and masonry. Just make sure the old walls are flat and have an adequate nailing area.

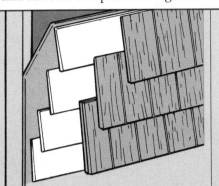

Residing over Beveled Siding. Begin with a double-starter course. Then nail the shingles to the high points of the bevels of each course. Use normal application techniques to complete the job.

Adding Shingles over Brick. Install vertical two-by furring to masonry walls using masonry nails at 16-inch intervals. Fasten 1×4 furring horizontally; space at intervals equal to the exposure you have chosen. Begin with a double starter course.

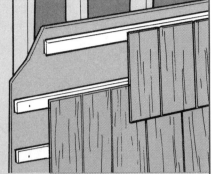

Covering Stucco with Shingles. Install horizontal 1×4 furring strips. Nail through the stucco and into the framing at least 1½ inches. Do not fur over stucco that is too cracked to remain stable.

Applying Double-Course Shingles

To cut costs and gain the effect of deep shadows, apply shingles and shakes in double courses. This technique exposes most of the higher-grade shingles and overlaps the less expensive shingles. The result is deep courses that provide excellent weather protection.

The maximum weather exposure manufacturers recommend for #1-grade shingles varies depending upon their size: 12 inches for 16-inch shingles, 14 inches for 18-inch shingles and 16 inches for 24-inch shingles. Shakes that are 18 inches long may be installed at exposures up to 14 inches; 24-inch shakes up to 18 inches.

1 Tripling the Starter Course.
The starter course actually is three layers. Use the less expensive #3-grade wood for the first two layers, and all subsequent undercourse layers. The third (face course) layer must extend 1/2 inch below the butt of the first two layers.

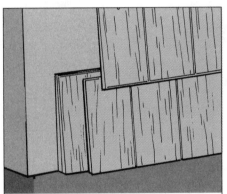

1 Begin the starter course with two layers of shingles. Install final layer 1/2 in. below butt edge.

2 Nailing the Double Course.
Use 6d galvanized casing nails to nail shingles 2 inches above the butt line and ¾ inch from both edges. Nail undercourse shingles with one nail about 2 inches from the top edge. The face course nails penetrate these shingles.

3 Adding Courses. Use a 1×4 tacked along the butt line as a guide. Undercourse shingles rest on the tops of the face shingles of the previous course.

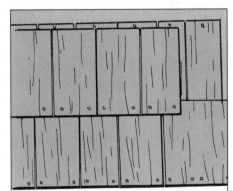

2 Nail shingles 2 in. above the butt line and 3/4 in. from both edges.

3 Undercourse shingles rest on the top edges of the face shingles of the previous course.

Corner Treatments

When cutting shingles for inside and outside corners, keep in mind the following rules of thumb:

■ Cuts parallel to the shingle edge can be made by splitting with a utility knife (angled cuts and crosscuts must be made with a saw).

■ For woven outside corners, alternate the overlap and rough-trim the shingles to fit.

■ Use a block plane to fine-tune one course at a time.

■ Use a table saw for forming mitered corners.

Cutting Angles for Gables

The T-bevel is the best tool for cutting shingles and shakes to the correct angle under gables. Use it to capture the angle and then mark the correct cut line. As with all angle and crosscuts, use a fine-toothed handsaw or circular saw equipped with a combination blade.

1 **Capturing the Angle.** Use the first whole shingle in the course as a plumb edge for setting the T-bevel. Cut a shingle and trim to achieve the necessary offset gap.

1 Use a T-bevel to capture the angle under gable eaves.

Corner Treatments

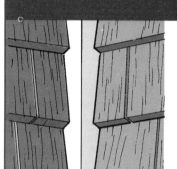

Inside Post. Trim shingles to abut a 2×2 post nailed to the inside corner.

Woven Inside. Eliminate the post and alternate the overlap of shingle edges at each course.

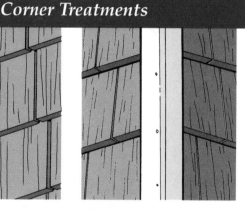

Trimmed Outside. Add one-by corner trim and butt shingles against it.

Woven Outside. Alternate the outside edge overlap with each course.

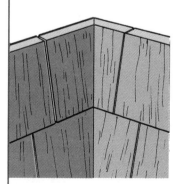

Mitered Inside. Use shingles mitered to fit in the corner. Start in the corner and work away from it as each course is added.

Mitered Outside. Use a table saw to cut miters. Match them up as courses are added. A difficult, but neat, trim approach.

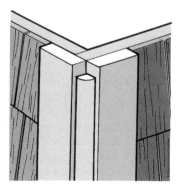

Trim and Quarter-Round Outside. Use quarter-round molding in the junction between two one-by pieces of trim. Butt shingles against the trim.

Frieze Trim. Overlay shingles with 1×6 or 1×8 boards. Cove molding eliminates attaching short pieces of shingles.

2 Use an off-cut as a template for trimming angled shingles.

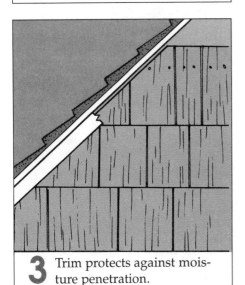

3 Trim protects against moisture penetration.

2 **Creating a Template.** After double-checking to make sure the angle is correct, keep the trimmed shingle as a template for cutting others.

3 **Overlapping Angles.** A piece of trim installed over the angled pieces adds protection against moisture infiltration as well as covers flaws.

Panelized Shingles

Prebonded wood shingle panels speed up installation dramatically. They are available in 8-foot-long panels with exposures that range from 4½ inches (4-course panels) to 14 inches (single-course panels). The shingles have a realistic gap

that does not reveal the plywood backing which is set at the butt line so that one panel is notched easily on top of another. Manufactured corners save time and make a clean finish to the wall.

The panels can be fastened directly to studs after building paper is applied (check local codes). They also can be applied to sheathing or furring strips. Colored galvanized nails usually are provided by the manufacturer. Staples are not recommended though some power nailers can be used.

1 **Installing Starter Strip.** Level a plywood starter strip along the lower edge of the wall. Be sure the strip is at least 6 inches above ground and leave room for the corner piece. The strip must be 1/2 inch thick and about 1 inch shorter than the exposure of each panel course. Insert two nails, one above the other, into each framing member along the length of the starter strip.

2 **Installing the Corner.** Place a corner piece even with the bottom edge of the starter strip. Check both sides for plumb. Face nail the corner, adding a nail 1/2 inch from the butt edge and 3/4 inch from each side. Don't bury the nail. Complete nailing by adding a nail at both top corners, 3/4 inch down from the top edge and 1/2 inch from each side.

Panelized Shingles. Imitate the look of wood shingles, but speed installation dramatically.

3 **Installing the Starter Course.** Butt one end of the panel against the corner. Leave a 1/16 inch gap. Make sure the bottom edge is even with the bottom edge of the starter strip.

1 Install a 1/2-in. thick starter strip at least 6 in. above ground level.

2 Install a corner piece even with the bottom edge of the starter strip.

3 Slip the first starter panel in place; leave a 1/16-in. gap where the panel joins the corner.

4 Nail the panel at every wall stud. Position nails 3/4 in. from the bottom edge. Nail from one end to the other to avoid cupping the panel.

5 A simple guide made of a square piece of plywood and a scrap of wood will help cut panels squarely.

6 Add the second and subsequent courses, nailing at each wall stud 3/4 in. from the butt edge.

7 Rip cut panels to a height that will fit under the eaves. Nail at the top and bottom.

4 **Nailing the Panels.** Do not bow or otherwise force panels into place. Allow 1/16 inch where panels meet, 1/8 inch where they abut windows, doors or trim. Nail from one end to the other at each stud, 3/4 inches from the bottom edge.

5 **Cutting Panels.** Use a circular saw with a combination blade to saw panels from behind (to reduce splintering). To ensure a square, even cut, make a simple guide from a square piece of plywood and a scrap of 1×2 or 1×3. Screw the one-by scrap to the edge of the plywood and then hook it over the edge of the panel to guide the saw.

6 **Adding Courses.** Check the first course for level. Face nail along the bottom, 3/4 inch from the edge, working across the panel a minimum of every 24 inches. Use 7d galvanized box nails. (If it has wavered slightly, strike a chalk line as a guide for aligning the tops of the second course panels.) Continue adding full courses.

7 **Topping It Off.** Rip cut the panels for the courses that butt the eaves. For gable ends, capture the angle and layout cuts as described in "Cutting Angles for Gables," page 54.

PAINTING & FINISHING WOOD SIDING

Preserve all the time and money you have invested in your siding job, by finishing it the right way. Though there are an impressive array of long-lasting paints and stains at your service, mistakes in application shorten the life of the finish and lead to time-consuming scraping and repainting. When it comes to finishing the job, there are many options.

Preparing to Paint

Whether you are replacing a few pieces of siding or residing the entire house, it is important to protect the new wood with primer and paint.

Priming the Wood. The job of primer is to seal the surface, hide imperfections and stains, and improve paint adhesion. Use a primer that is compatible with the final coat you will be using. Oil-based primer suits both water- and oil-based topcoats. Water-based primer is generally topped only with a water-based topcoat. Be sure the surface being primed is clean of dirt and dust to ensure adhesion.

Applying Paint. Two coats of paint provide the longest-lasting results, particularly on the south and west sides of the house where the sun is most intense. Weigh the advantages yourself: One coat of paint over a primed surface lasts about 5 years; two coats lasts up to 10 years. Apply the first coat no later than two weeks after priming and the second coat when the first coat is dry.

Avoiding Common Mistakes

- Never paint in the rain.

- Make sure the surface is clean and dry.

- Do not paint when the wall is hot or in direct sunlight.

- Use a mildewcide to remove mildew. Do not simply paint over mildew, as it will grow under the paint and cause blistering.

- Paint at temperatures no lower than 50°F for latex paint and 40°F for oil-based paint.

Choosing Paints and Stains

PAINT OR STAIN	MAKEUP	SPECIAL USE	STRENGTHS	LIMITATIONS
Primer	Water based	Before oil- or water-based topcoat	Increases adhesion	Not intended as final coat
Primer	Oil based	Before oil- or water-based topcoat	Increases adhesion, seals wood	Not intended as final coat
Alkyd	Oil (often linseed), mineral spirits, pigment, alkyd resin	Needs no primer over prepainted surfaces	Long lasting	Cleanup requires mineral spirits
Latex	Acrylic or alkyd resin, pigment, water	Needs no primer over prepainted surfaces	Easy cleanup with soap and water	Less permanent than alkyd
Penetrating Stain	Alkyd or oil based, fungicide, water repellent	Where wood grain is desirable	Has no surface film to blister or crack	Not for covering solid-color stain or old paint
Solid-Color Stain	Heavy pigment content, alkyd or oil based, fungicide, water repellent	Rough surfaces	Tends to chalk rather than peel	Can have paint-like film that will blister
Wood Preservative	Fungicide, water repellent, resin, solvent	Bare or stripped wood before priming, especially at butt joints and in corners	Long life due to minimal surface film	Paint will not adhere to some; check before purchasing

Using a Caulk Gun

1. Twist the plunger to release the ratchet and pull back. Tip the rear of the cartridge into the barrel and push the cartridge into the barrel. Pull the trigger gently a couple of times to settle the cartridge in place.

2. Use a utility knife to cut the nozzle at a 45-degree angle. If you need a wide opening cut farther back on the nozzle. A foil seal protects the caulk. Use a long nail to puncture the seal.

3. Hold the gun at a 45-degree angle to the opening. Position it so that as you draw the gun steadily along, the caulk is applied to both sides of the opening. Squeeze the trigger firmly to maintain a steady bead.

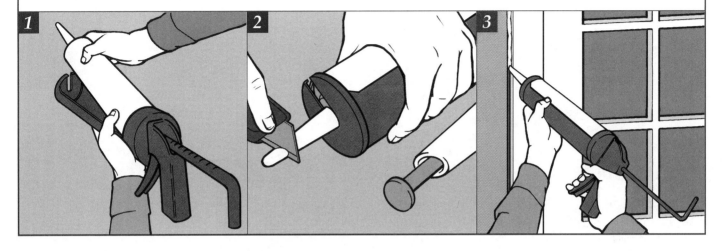

Painting Techniques

Among finish options, paint offers the longest-lived protection and the greatest range of colors. There probably is no other do-it-yourself job that yields such dramatic results for a relatively small investment in materials.

Begin painting at the highest point and work your way down the wall.

Spread dropcloths to protect the foundation and plants. Start with the siding and finish with the trim.

Preparing the Paint

1 Pouring the Paint. Begin by pouring the watery top layer of liquid into a clean one-gallon container. Set it aside.

2 Stirring the Pigment. A thick paste remains at the bottom of the bucket. Use a piece of clean 1×2 to break up lumps. Stir the paste using a figure-eight motion and finish with a quick, lifting stir.

3 Putting the Two Together. While stirring, slowly pour in the liquid originally set aside.

1 Pour the thin watery layer of paint into a clean container.

2 Break up lumps as you stir the remaining paste in a figure-eight motion.

3 Combine the two, slowly pouring in the watery part while stirring.

4 **Boxing the Paint.** When the job requires more than one gallon of paint, professional painters "box" the paint by mixing several gallons together to ensure uniform color. Box enough paint to cover at least one side of the house. If there is leftover paint, box it along with the paint prepared for the next side of the house.

5 **Eliminating Drippy Cans.** Puncture the deepest part of the lip of the bucket with a nail so that excess paint drains into the bucket rather than down the side of the can.

4 Box enough paint to coat one whole side of the house.

5 Use a nail to puncture the lip of the can.

Brushing on Paint & Stain

1 **Covering the Lap.** When working with beveled siding, begin by painting the underside of the courses. Use a 4-inch brush. Press out excess paint on the inside of the can so it does not run down the brush handle while you work. When finished, check the undersides of the courses from the ground. It is easier to detect skipped areas from below.

2 **Working with the Grain.** Using the same brush apply the paint with short, quick strokes following the direction of the grain. Then work paint into fissures, smoothing it. Feather the end of the section with light strokes so it melds with the next area to be painted.

3 **Painting the Window Sash.** Use a 1½-inch tapered-trim brush to paint the window sash. After painting the top portion, open the window a few inches. This breaks paint seals and prevents painting the window closed.

1 Use a 4-in. brush to paint the undersides of the siding. Occasionally check coverage from the ground.

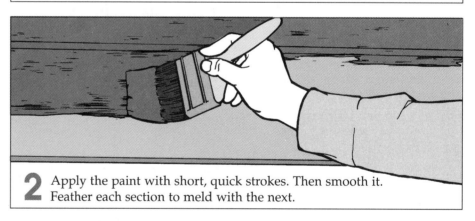

2 Apply the paint with short, quick strokes. Then smooth it. Feather each section to meld with the next.

3 Use a 1½-in. brush to paint the window sash. Take care not to paint the window shut.

Cleaning up Brushes

The major advantage to using latex paint is the easy cleanup. A brush used for latex paint or stain need only be washed thoroughly with soap and water, rinsed and slapped back and forth until nearly dry. Brushes used with oil-based paint and stain require more attention.

1 **Soaking Thinner.** Press away excess paint with a scraper or paint stirrer. Then soak the brush in thinner, working the bristles against the bottom of the container. To remove paint deep in the bristles massage the brush (especially up near the handle).

2 **Drying the Brush.** Press out excess thinner and twirl the brush inside a container. Repeat procedure until the brush is as clean as possible.

3 **Combing the Brush.** Comb the bristles, making sure to get at the bristles in the center of the brush. Hang the brush from its handle to dry.

4 **Wrapping for Storage.** After brushes are dry, wrap them in newspaper to keep the bristles flat and straight. Fold the newspaper so that it wraps the bristles, but does not bend them. Tape it and store it flat.

1 Soak the brush in thinner. Work the thinner into the bristles.

2 Press out the excess thinner and then twirl the brush.

3 Comb the bristles with a wire brush. Hang the brush to dry.

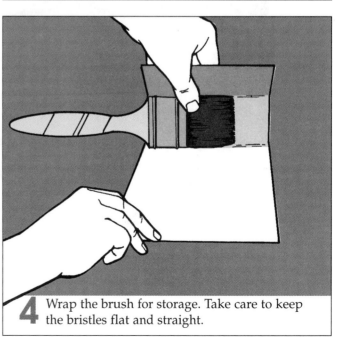

4 Wrap the brush for storage. Take care to keep the bristles flat and straight.

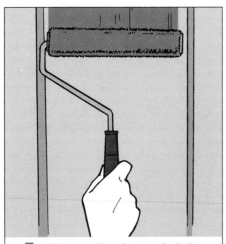

1 Use a roller that is slightly narrower than the area to be covered.

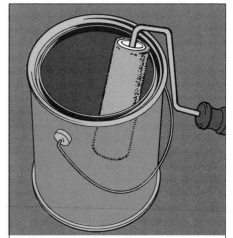

2 Speciality rollers reach into corners.

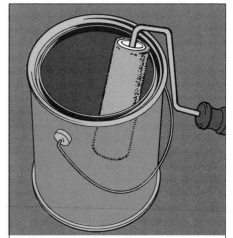

3 Suspend the roller so the side of the roller cover is not flattened.

Painting & Staining with Rollers

Use a roller to apply paint quickly and evenly. It will leave a stippled textured that becomes more pronounced with deeper naps. Rollers are ideal for covering rough or deeply textured siding. Usually a small brush is needed for covering hard-to-get-to areas.

1 **Rolling the Flats.** When covering horizontal or vertical planks choose a roller to suit the width of the planks. On other surfaces use a standard-width roller. Apply paint first by rolling opposite to the grain, then smooth by rolling with the grain.

2 **Rolling in Corners.** Specialty rollers are needed to reach into corners and along trim. Keep a small brush handy to get to especially awkward spots.

3 **Cleaning Roller Covers.** Soak the roller under running water and then squeeze out the paint from one end to the other. Hang the roller by the handle so the cover dries evenly.

Painting & Staining with Pads

Painting pads provide quick, smooth coverage and can reach into moderate textures.

1 **Reaching under Laps.** Run a paint- or stain-loaded pad under courses. Use long strokes.

2 **Covering Siding Faces.** Choose a pad as close as possible to the siding exposures to help you get by with the least number of strokes.

3 **Covering Textures.** Pads specially designed for grained textures are available.

1 Cover the underside of the course with the pad first.

2 Use a pad with the same exposure as the siding.

3 Speciality pads reach deeply into grained textures.

SELECTING & INSTALLING VINYL SIDING

Speed of installation, low maintenance, and damage resistance have made vinyl siding more popular than ever. Once plainly utilitarian, today vinyl siding is available in a wide variety of styles with textures and trim accessories to suit each one. Although often left to the professionals, the job of installing siding is well within the range of experienced do-it-yourselfers.

New Designs in Vinyl

Vinyl siding, with near-zero maintenance demands, can make home ownership less of a full-time occupation. Life expectancy for vinyl siding is up to 40 years. Vinyl once was considered a low-maintenance, but bland, siding material that covered all architectural details of the house. These days you can find a wide range of styles, sizes and architectural features true to your home.

The vinyl itself varies in thickness and sheen. Most homeowners prefer a low sheen that resembles painted wood. Builder's grade vinyl (.040 gauge) is very glossy. Mid-range siding (.042–.044) offers additional profiles. Premium and reinforced grades add extra thickness and design options with low sheen.

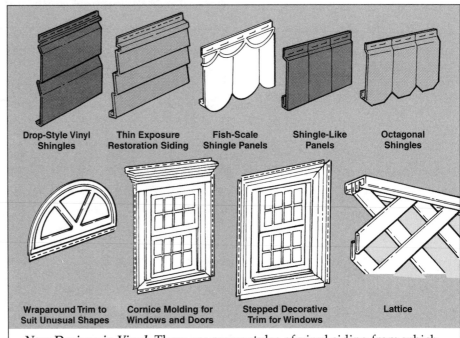

Drop-Style Vinyl Shingles   Thin Exposure Restoration Siding   Fish-Scale Shingle Panels   Shingle-Like Panels   Octagonal Shingles

Wraparound Trim to Suit Unusual Shapes   Cornice Molding for Windows and Doors   Stepped Decorative Trim for Windows   Lattice

New Designs in Vinyl. There are many styles of vinyl siding from which to choose. Pick the one that best suits the style of your home.

Retrimming Doors & Windows

Residing, furring, and insulating over old siding all add inches to the walls. If the added depth is not taken into account at openings, the junction between new siding and existing windows and doors will leak.

1 Building the Jamb. Use a pry bar to pry exterior casing gently from window or door jambs. Score the joints along the casing to break the paint seal and avoid splintering.

2 Adding Extender Strip. Nail an extender strip flush with the inside of side and top jambs. The strip must be thick enough to bring the jamb edge even with the existing wall surface. Rip a piece of one-by that is equal to the width of the casing. Butt side strips against the top piece and trim lower ends to the angle of the sill. Nail with 6d galvanized box nails.

3 Nailing the Casing. If the old casing is in good condition, remove the nails and use 8d galvanized box nails to reinstall it later. If need be, cut new brick mold instead. The casing must be set back 1/8 inch from the inside (window) edge of the extension piece.

Casing

1 Carefully pry off old molding before extending window casing.

Extender Strip

2 Nail an extender strip of ample thickness onto the jamb so that the jamb is even with the old wall surface.

3 Use 8d galvanized nails to nail casing. Cut new pieces to size or reuse the old.

4 **Installing the Drip Cap.** Mount a prefabricated drip flashing or use roll flashing to make one yourself. (Fold a 1/2-inch lip over the top casing, cover its top and carry the flashing 3 inches up the wall.) Nail it along the top edge only.

5 **Extending the Sill.** Plane the nose of a rounded sill flat and square. Add bullnose molding to extend the sill. Fasten it with exterior glue and 8d galvanized box nails.

Basic Installation Techniques

The installation of vinyl, accounting for 40 percent or more of a contractor's cost, is within the skill range of do-it-yourselfers. Although many vinyl siding styles are available today, the only significant installation differences depend on whether you are using horizontal or vertical siding panels. Both types use modular, lock-together trim and panels that are designed to allow vinyl to expand and contract with temperature changes. These modular systems cover minor mistakes. The systems are a bit different, but require the same nailing and cutting techniques.

Nailing Vinyl

Nails do not so much fasten vinyl as hang it. In fact, if you think of vinyl as a living thing always needing room to move, you are on the right track.

Nailing Slots. With very few exceptions, hammer nails only through precut slots. To allow for movement both ways, always place the nail in the center of the slot.

Nailing Straight. Keep the nail at a 90-degree angle. Do not angle downward or toenail.

Nailing Loose. Nail just far enough so that a slight gap remains between the nailhead and the vinyl. Leave a gap of 1/32 inch (about the thickness of a matchbook cover).

4 Install a metal or vinyl drip cap over the casing.

5 Plane the sill flat and add an extension.

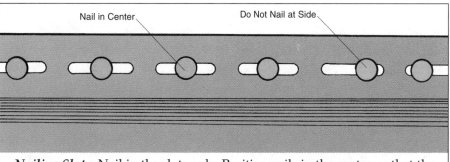

Nailing Slots. Nail in the slots only. Position nails in the center so that the siding can move in both directions.

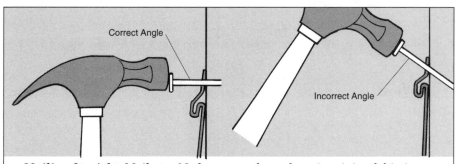

Nailing Straight. Nail at a 90-degree angle so there is minimal friction as the panel slides.

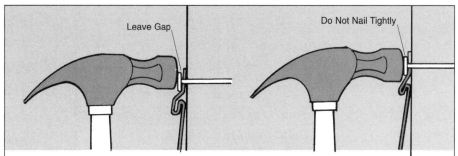

Nailing Loose. Nail just far enough to leave a gap of 1/32 in. (the thickness of a matchbook) between the nailhead and the siding.

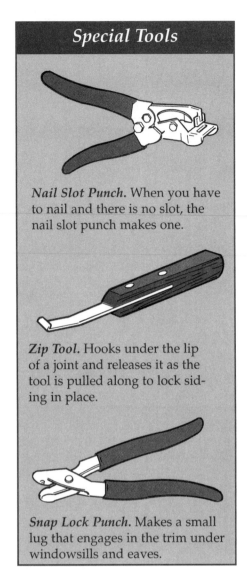

Nail Slot Punch. When you have to nail and there is no slot, the nail slot punch makes one.

Zip Tool. Hooks under the lip of a joint and releases it as the tool is pulled along to lock siding in place.

Snap Lock Punch. Makes a small lug that engages in the trim under windowsills and eaves.

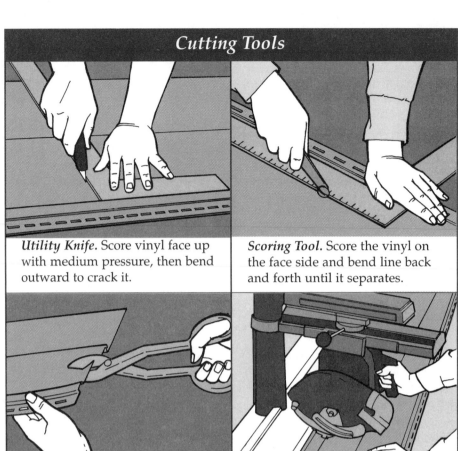

Utility Knife. Score vinyl face up with medium pressure, then bend outward to crack it.

Scoring Tool. Score the vinyl on the face side and bend line back and forth until it separates.

Tin Snips. For a clean, smooth cut, do not completely close the blades at the end of a cut.

Power Saw with Reverse Blade. Reverse a fine-tooth blade (12 to 16 teeth per inch) to saw vinyl.

Caution: Do not use the same saw for cutting wood while the blade is reversed.

Installing Siding

Whether you are adding vertical or horizontal siding, the foundation for a quality siding job is a straight, solid nailing base. Sheathing that has been cleared of all siding makes the best base. However, rigid insulation board or furring strips over sound siding also are good surfaces for new siding. Old vinyl, aluminum or steel siding is not solid enough to take a nail and must be removed before the new vinyl is installed. Stucco and masonry surfaces must be leveled with furring strips nailed over them.

Installing Channels & Corners

Once the foundation is ready, you can install channel and siding pieces.

1 Striking a Guideline. Run a line level along the entire length of the wall at the bottom edge of the sheathing. If you find one corner is lower than the other, measure up 1¾ inches from that corner and strike a chalk line at that point.

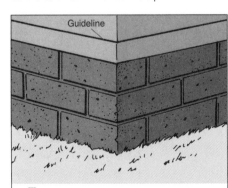

1 Strike a guideline for the starter strip.

2 Attaching Starter Strip. Use the slots provided to fasten the starter strip in place. Nail only to within 1/32 inch of the vinyl surface. Allow space for inside and outside corner posts and J-channel around windows and doors. When abutting

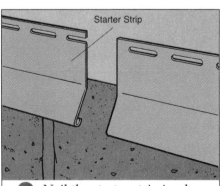

2 Nail the starter strip in place using the nailing slots.

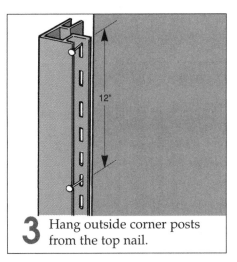

3 Hang outside corner posts from the top nail.

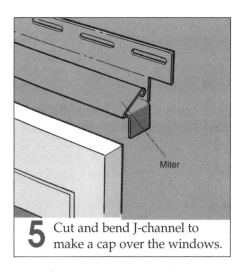

4 Add inside corner posts.

Corner Post

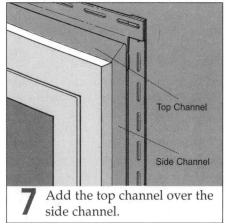

5 Cut and bend J-channel to make a cap over the windows.

Miter

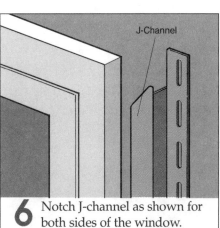

6 Notch J-channel as shown for both sides of the window.

J-Channel

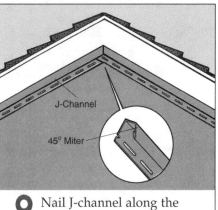

7 Add the top channel over the side channel.

Top Channel

Side Channel

8 Attach undersill trim to wood furring.

Window Casing

J-Channel

Window Sill

Undersill Trim

Furring

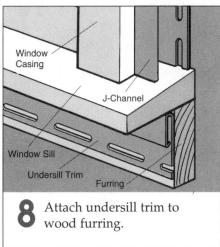

9 Nail J-channel along the gables so the siding edges slip into it.

J-Channel

45° Miter

two starter strips leave 1/4 inch between them.

3 Attaching Outside Corner Posts. Hang corner posts. Nail into the topmost slot so that the top of the post is 1/4 inch from the top of the wall. The topmost nail is an exception to the rule: It touches the top of the slot. Nail the post, working downward. Be sure to nail straight on and in the center of the slot only. Drive nails at 12-inch intervals.

4 Adding Inside Corner Posts. Inside corner posts are installed the same way outside corner posts are installed. Leave 1/4 inch at the top for expansion and nail all but the top nail in the center of each slot.

5 Sealing Window & Door Tops. J-channel is cut and shaped to wrap and cap side pieces over windows and doors. Cut the front of the J-channel at a 45-degree angle for a mitered appearance. Cut along the bends and bend a lip that wraps over the side pieces.

6 Sealing Window Sides. Install side pieces. Notch them so that a tab from the top J-channel overlaps and creates a weather-tight joint.

7 Capping Windows. Nail the side pieces of J-channel in place. (With J-channels you do not have to be concerned with

expansion.) Place the top piece of J-channel so the bent tab wraps around the side piece.

8 Attaching Undersill Trim. Nail a wood furring strip under the window sill to maintain the angle of the siding. Nail undersill trim to the strip.

9 Attaching J-Channel Beneath Gables. Fasten J-channel beneath the eaves so that the edge of the siding slips into it. Nail at 6- to 12-inch intervals. Miter the edge that overlaps at the peak.

Installing Horizontal Siding

After the channels and corners are prepared, the job proceeds at a quick pace.

1 Adding the First Course. Hook the piece of siding under the starter strip and push up on the butt to lock it in place. Nail in such a way that the siding is not overly stretched. Nail every 16 inches. Unlike wood siding, junctions between sections of siding do not have to fall directly over wall studs.

2 Overlapping for Appearance. Choose the preferred vantage points from which your house is viewed, such as the front entrance, driveway and deck area. Where there are vertical joints between panels, make sure the panels that are nearer the vantage point overlap the panels that are further away. This will make the joints less visible from the preferred vantage points.

3 Lapping Panel Joints. Overlap end joints 1 inch and notch the nailing flange at the end of cut panels another 1/2 to 1 inch to allow for expansion. Try to duplicate the factory end notch. Avoid joints over doors and windows. Stagger joints by 4 feet horizontally and at least two courses vertically.

4 Siding Around Openings. To fit a panel around a window or door, mark the width of the notch by holding the panel in place. Add 1/4 inch to both sides for expansion. Make a template from a short scrap of siding. Lock the template into the course nearest the window and mark the depth. Add 1/4 inch and transfer the mark to the piece of siding to be cut.

5 Joining Siding Under Windowsills. As you notch the siding to fit under the window, slip the notch into the undersill trim and lock the piece into the course below. For "picture frame" windows that have molding all around instead of a windowsill, install J-molding at the bottom, joining it to the side J-molding just as you did at top. Then install undersill trim inside the bottom J-molding as show in step 7 "Anchoring the Panel" on page 71.

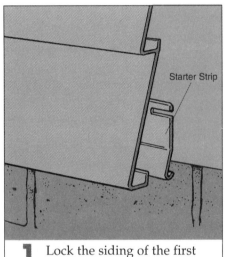

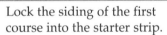

1 Lock the siding of the first course into the starter strip.

2 Overlap siding away from main entrances.

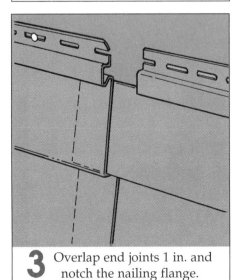

3 Overlap end joints 1 in. and notch the nailing flange.

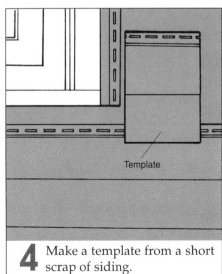

4 Make a template from a short scrap of siding.

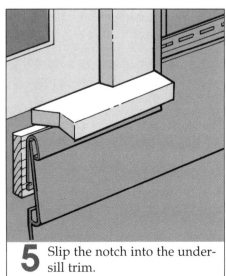

5 Slip the notch into the undersill trim.

6 Cutting for Openings. Make vertical cuts with tin snips and horizontal cuts with a utility knife or scorer guided by a straightedge. Once scored, bow the area outward to break it.

7 Mounting Undersill Trim at Eaves. Nail undersill trim along the top of the wall at the eaves. Because only the top edge of the siding meets the eaves, undersill trim is used instead of J-channel. Measure the distance between it and the last siding course. Check measurements at several points. You may have to taper the piece to fit.

8 Cutting the Last Course. Use a utility knife or scorer to mark the siding trim lengthwise. The cut need not be perfectly straight because the undersill trim covers imperfections.

9 Punching Lugs. The snap lock punch makes lugs that grab under the undersill trim to hold the upper part of the siding panel in place. Make a lug every 6 to 12 inches.

10 Fitting the Panel. Push the upper edge of final panel into the undersill trim as the bottom edge is locked into the course below.

11 Fitting at Gable Peaks. To mark the gable slope on siding panels, make a gable template. Position a piece of scrap onto the siding course below and hold a second piece of scrap against the J-channel mounted at the gable. Mark the first piece of scrap as a template. Cut it and test the fit. Write the word "SAVE" on it and use it for other gable cuts. The last triangle in the peak must be cut to size, locked in place and nailed at its peak.

6 Use tin snips to start the notch. Finish by scoring and breaking the siding.

7 Measure the distance between the inside of the undersill trim and the last siding course.

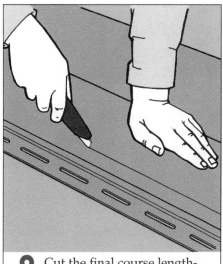

8 Cut the final course lengthwise by scoring and snapping.

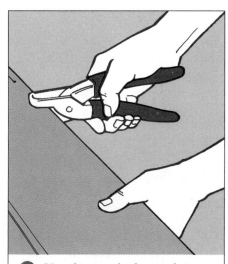

9 Use the snaplock punch to cut locking tabs every 6 to 12 in.

10 Push the top of the final piece into the undersill trim until lugs and the bottom lock in place.

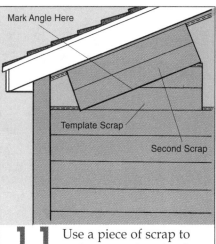

Mark Angle Here

Template Scrap

Second Scrap

11 Use a piece of scrap to make a template for the gable angle. Cut the angle and save for future use.

Installing Vertical Siding

The cutting and nailing of vertical siding does not differ from that of horizontal siding, but the accessory pieces do. This is because vertical siding has channels that are necessary for rigidity. They require a deeper, shelf-like starter strip called head flashing. In addition, they may intersect window, doors and corners at full thickness, or where there is a vertical channel. The methods needed for joining and sealing the siding at vertical junctures vary considerably.

Before installing vertical vinyl siding, you must provide a sound nailing surface. This may be a sound wall or a horizontal 1×3 furring nailed every 12 inches to wall studs.

1 Marking a Guideline. Typically a chalk line is struck 1 inch above the lowest corner of the sheathing (check the manufacturer's instructions).

2 Adding Corners. When measuring for the corner pieces, use a scrap of head flashing held at the guideline to help mark the corners so they are 1/4 to 1/2 inch below the head flashing. Hang corner pieces by a nail in the topmost slot 1/4 inch from the soffit above. Nail every 6 to 12 inches down the corner, placing nails in the center of the slots.

3 Installing Head Flashing. Once the corners are in place cut and nail the head flashing. Position it so the nailing slots line up with the guideline. Overlap pieces by 1/2 inch, trimming off the back an additional 1/2 inch for expansion. Install head flashing over windows and doors as well.

4 Attaching J-Channel. Install J-channel along the top of gables and eaves.

5 Wrapping Windows and Doors. Surround windows with J-channel. The top piece covers the flashing and is notched so that a tab overlaps the side channel. Do the same underneath the window; leave a tab that fits into the J-channel beneath the sill.

6 Installing Vertical Starter Strips. Measure and mark the center of the wall. Nail the vertical starter strip plumb with the mark. Nail it as you did the corners. Vertical starter strip is designed to accept panels from both sides.

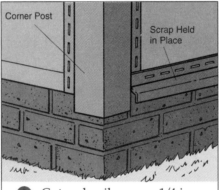

1 Strike a level chalk line 1 in. above the lowest corner of the sheathing.

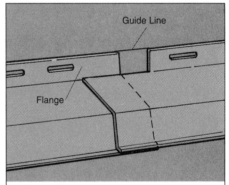

2 Cut and nail corners 1/4 in. below the soffit and 1/4 to 1/2 in. below the bottom of the head flashing.

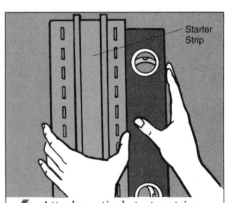

3 Attach the head flashing so that nailing slot flanges are under the guideline. Overlap pieces by 1/2 in.

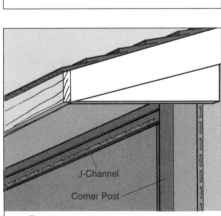

4 Install J-channel under all eaves and gables.

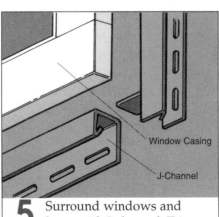

5 Surround windows and doors with J-channel. Trim and wrap corners as shown.

6 Attach vertical starter strips centered at each wall.

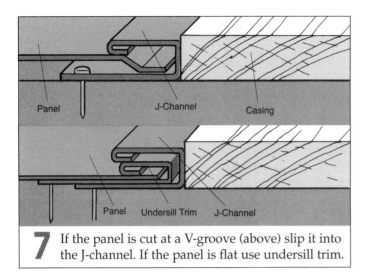

7 If the panel is cut at a V-groove (above) slip it into the J-channel. If the panel is flat use undersill trim.

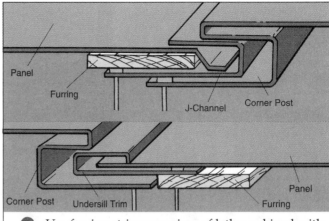

8 Use furring strips or a piece of lath combined with J-channel or undersill trim to lock in the panels.

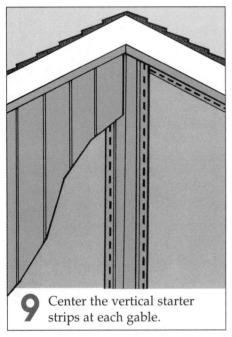

9 Center the vertical starter strips at each gable.

7 **Anchoring the Panel.** The panel is cut either at a V-groove or on the flat of the panel. If the cut is at the V-groove, simply slip it into the J-channel. If the cut is on the flat of the panel, install undersill trim in the J-channel to sandwich the panel in place.

8 **Anchoring Panels at a Corner.** Sometimes the V-groove of a panel is inserted into a corner piece and sometimes it is inserted into the flat portion of the panel. Both must be sandwiched and held in place at the corner. Use furring strips or pieces of lath combined with J-channel or undersill trim to lock in the panels.

9 **Centering Starter Strips.** Trim the end of a vertical starter strip and nail it in place so it touches the apex of the gable. Plumb it and then trim it so it sits in the J-channel at the base of gable. Install panels beginning at the vertical starter strip. Lock panels in place and nail every 6 to 12 inches. Each panel is cut 1/4 inch short of touching the inside of the top J-channel (see page 66).

Installing Soffits & Fascia

Vinyl soffits and fascia complete the job. For most soffits the approach is straightforward: A piece called the "F-channel" (which is an "F" in profile) is nailed to the wall beneath the eaves or gable and to the underside of the fascia edge. Soffit panels are cut to width and slipped into the F-channel. The fascia is covered with pieces that hook onto the bottom of the F-channel and lock into undersill trim just beneath the roofing. Finally, trim pieces are added.

1 **Attaching F-Channel to Fascia.** F-channel is nailed through the slots to the fascia every 6 to 12 inches.

2 **Attaching F-Channel to Wall.** Use a spirit level to mark the wall at points that are level with the bottom edge of the F-channel. Strike a line and nail the F-channel in place.

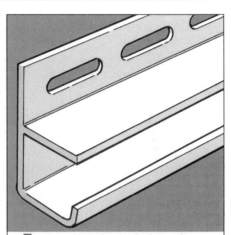

1 Install F-channel along the bottom of the fascia. Nail in the center of slots every 6 to 12 in.

2 Strike a guideline and nail F-channel along the wall.

Soffit Panel

3 Slip panels into the F-channels starting at a corner.

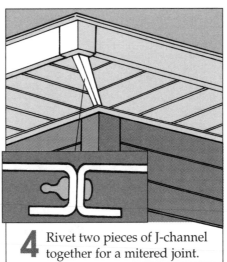

4 Rivet two pieces of J-channel together for a mitered joint.

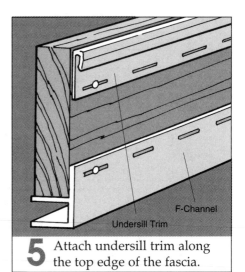

F-Channel

Undersill Trim

5 Attach undersill trim along the top edge of the fascia.

3 Cutting and Inserting Panels. Cut panel sections to the width needed minus 1/4 inch. Slip them into the channels, loading them from one end of the soffit.

4 Mitering at Corners. To support the mitered joint in the places where panels meet at corners use a pop riveter to join two pieces of J-channel. For gable returns continue the soffit to the gable fascia and use doubled J-channel to make the transition.

5 Covering Fascia. Attach undersill trim along the top of the old fascia and F-channel along the bottom, nailing every 6 to 12 inches. Allow for expansion by cutting trim 1/4 inch less than the length of the fascia.

6 Adding Lugs to Fascia Cover. Cut a length of fascia cover to the necessary width. Use a snap lock punch to add lugs along the top edge every 6 to 12 inches.

7 Installing Fascia Cover. Lock the fascia cover in place by inserting the upper edge into the finishing trim. At the same time hook the bottom of the fascia cover over the F-channel. Push upward so that the cover flange and the lugs lock into place.

6 Use a snaplock punch to add lugs every 6 to 12 in.

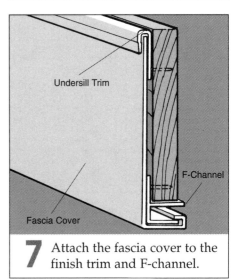

Undersill Trim

Fascia Cover

F-Channel

7 Attach the fascia cover to the finish trim and F-channel.

Evaluating a Contractor

Vinyl, as well as aluminum, often is installed by professionals. It is difficult to evaluate the best contractor for the job. What should a homeowner do once a contractor's estimates and references are in hand?

■ Make certain you are aware of the trim options offered and how the contractor plans to use them on your house.

■ Take the time to visit jobs the contractor has completed. Find a siding job comparable to that planned for your house. Check the wall for waves (horizontal) or bumps (vertical) in the siding. Waves and bumps indicate inadequate preparation of the base, improper nailing or slipshod furring.

■ Check for gaps that may have resulted from careless cutting of panels or haphazard nailing.

■ Laps must be staggered not clustered, and spaced in a way that minimizes their visibility.

■ Light fixtures, downspouts and shutters must be firmly attached. They must look as if they are attached to solid backing rather than just siding.

SELECTING & INSTALLING ALUMINUM SIDING

During the 40 years aluminum siding has been around, it has proven to be a durable, low-maintenance material. It continues to improve with an ever-increasing number of textures and siding profiles from which to choose. While aluminum is more difficult to cut and handle than vinyl, the installation remains within the grasp of a do-it-yourselfer. Though the component systems of the two materials are remarkably similar, there are some key ways in which they differ.

Avoiding Scratches. To prevent scratching, use a jig to keep the base of the saw off the siding. Use an aluminum-cutting blade with a minimum of 10 points.

Cutting with Caution. Cutting aluminum is more dangerous than cutting vinyl. Always wear goggles and gloves for protection against metal burrs and slivers.

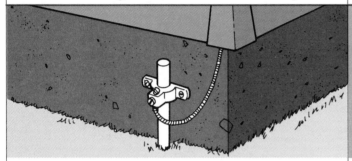

Grounding Aluminum. Most codes require that aluminum siding is grounded. Mount a #8 ground wire to a clip on one panel and route it to a grounding clamp that is attached to a cold water pipe or to a grounding stake.

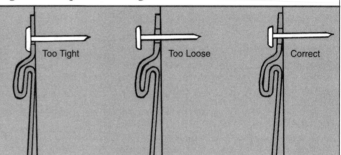

Allowing for Expansion and Contraction. Nail only in the center of each slot. Allow 1/16 inch between the nailhead and the surface of the aluminum. Use only aluminum nails to prevent deterioration of aluminum.

Getting Started

1 Covering Trim. Coil aluminum stock is available in a wide range of colors for covering trim. Make crisp corner bends by clamping the metal between two 1x4s before bending. You also can rent a break (the machine used by the professionals) to do the job. Start at the sill and work upward. This is the most difficult aspect of applying aluminum. You may opt to paint the trim and use siding only on the walls.

2 Preparing Windows. Add J-channel around the sides and tops of window and door casing. Tabs bent on the top piece of J-channel overlap side pieces protecting the wood from moisture damage. Nail all but the last 6 inches of the

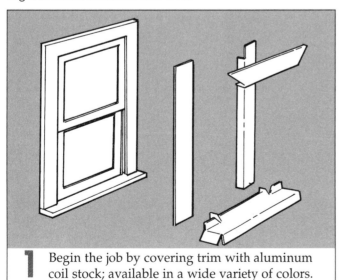

1 Begin the job by covering trim with aluminum coil stock; available in a wide variety of colors.

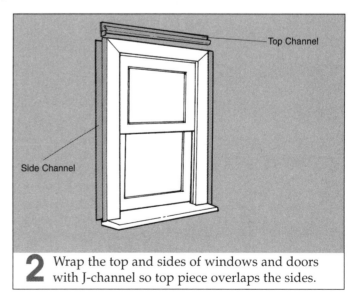

2 Wrap the top and sides of windows and doors with J-channel so top piece overlaps the sides.

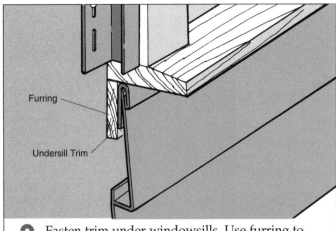

3 Fasten trim under windowsills. Use furring to keep the angle of the siding consistent.

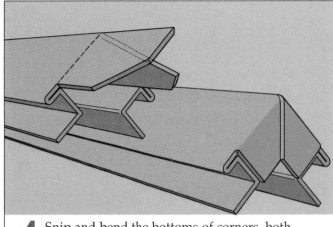

4 Snip and bend the bottoms of corners, both outside and inside, to make a cap.

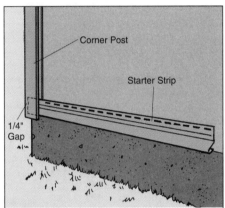

5 Leave a 1/4 in. gap between the end of starters strips and siding panels and the inside corner of corner post.

bottom ends of the side pieces so flashing can be added as the courses are installed.

3 **Furring and Trimming Beneath Sills.** Cut finish trim to go beneath the sill. As you work up the wall decide how much furring, if any, is necessary to keep the siding beneath the window consistent with the angle of the rest of the course.

4 **Capping Corners.** Aluminum holds a bend. Snip and bend the bottom of each corner post to seal and protect it from moisture and insects.

5 **Installing Starter Strips.** Nail the starter strip along a line leveled 1 inch from the top of the foundation.

Installing Horizontal Siding

Aluminum siding is not a pleasant material to work with, but its interlocking system is well thought out and easily learned. Once you under-stand the components, you can make quick progress. Like vinyl, aluminum moves with temperature changes so nail and overlap pieces accordingly.

The components, nailing procedures, and steps for installing aluminum siding are remarkably similar to those of vinyl. The only major difference in methods is that the zip tool used for vinyl is not used for aluminum. Instead, the lower edges of course panels hook, rather than lock, into the upper edges of the

previous course. One minor difference is that aluminum panels 8 inch deep or more require backer tabs at the joints. As with vinyl siding a snap lock punch is used occasionally under sills, soffits and eaves, and joints between panels overlap to allow for movement. Eaves and soffit treatments also are the same.

1 **Installing the First Course.** Hook the first piece of siding to the starter strip and nail. Be sure the end of the piece is 1/4 inch from the inside post. Nail at 16-inch intervals, leaving a 1/16-inch gap between the nailhead and the aluminum so that the piece hangs. Prepare the next panel by notching the nailing flange by 1½ inches so that the panels overlap by that amount.

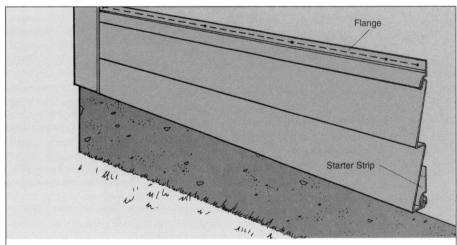

1 Hook the first course panels onto the starter strip and nail through flange every 16 in. Leave 1/16 in. between the nailhead and the siding surface.

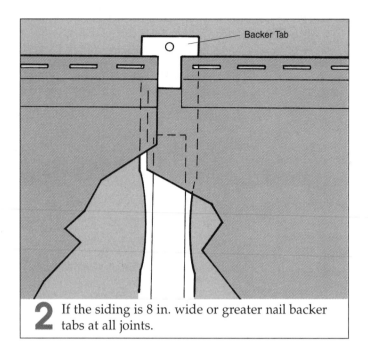

2 If the siding is 8 in. wide or greater nail backer tabs at all joints.

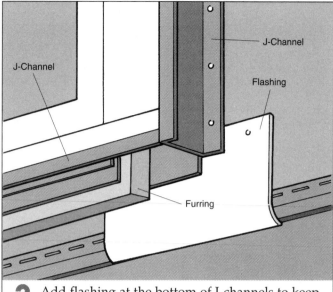

3 Add flashing at the bottom of J-channels to keep water from getting behind the siding.

2 **Installing Backer Tabs.** If you are using 8-inch or deeper siding, install backer tabs at each lap joint. Backer tabs keep the joint even and rigid. Nail backer tabs to the wall.

3 **Flashing at Windows.** Add flashing over the last full course before the window. Slip a square of aluminum under the J-channel so that its bottom edge just touches the bottom edge of the locking channel. Nail the flashing in place.

4 **Attaching Panels.** If needed, fur out the finish trim so the final course beneath the window does not bow inward.

5 **Furring above Windows and Doors.** Fur out a notched piece of siding by adding a wooden strip just thick enough to keep the angle of the siding consistent. Install finish trim over it, nailing at 16-inch intervals. Slip the notched siding in place and continue to add courses.

6 **Furring at Eaves.** Panels usually have to be cut horizontally to finish off a wall. If partial panels are used, fur them out before adding the undersill trim into which the cut edge fits.

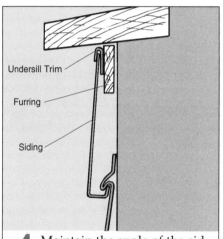

4 Maintain the angle of the siding by furring out the undersill trim where necessary.

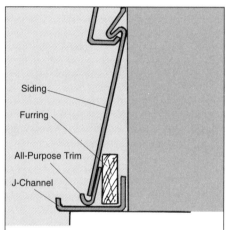

5 Add furrring above windows before adding finish trim and notching the next course.

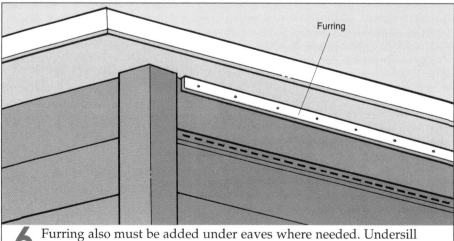

6 Furring also must be added under eaves where needed. Undersill trim combines with the locked base of the siding to hold it in place.

Notching & Flashing

Often aluminum is rigid enough that it does not have to be furred. There is a way to cleanly maintain the right siding angle without adding furring.

1 Making Initial Cuts. Hold the siding above the opening for which it will be notched. Mark the width plus 1/4 inch on each side. In addition, measure the height of the notch and add 1/4 inch. Use tin snips to make the vertical cuts.

2 Cutting Horizontally. Determine the amount needed to maintain the right angle, score a line and break off the scrap.

3 Bending the Tab. Place the piece over a 2×4 or 2×6 laid on sawhorses. Line up the edge of the wood with the line to bend. Then, bend the tab over the plank of wood.

Caution: *Wear protective gloves.*

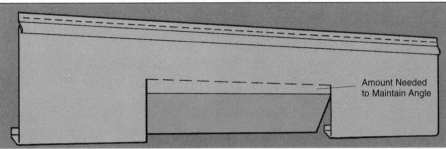

1 Mark the area to be notched. Allow an extra 1/4 in. on all sides.

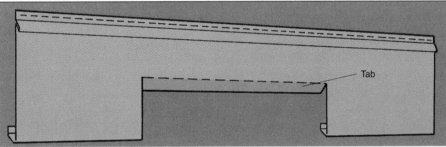

2 Determine the amount needed to maintain the right angle, measure down from the notched line, score and break away excess.

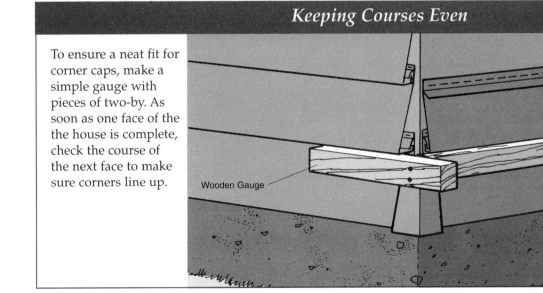

3 Using a 2×4 or 2×6 as a straightedge, bend the tab inward. Fasten the notch in place with its built-in furring.

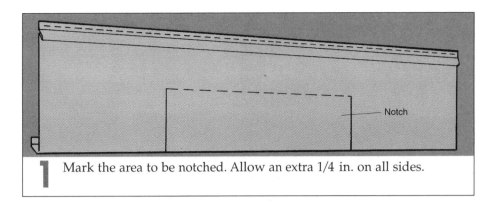

Keeping Courses Even

To ensure a neat fit for corner caps, make a simple gauge with pieces of two-by. As soon as one face of the the house is complete, check the course of the next face to make sure corners line up.

Wooden Gauge

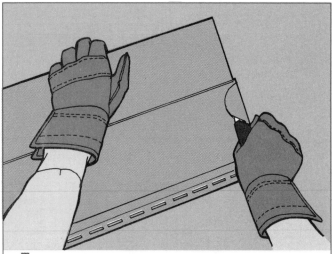

1 Cut a half-round hole for the faucet pipe. Make it 1/4 in. greater in diameter than the pipe to allow for expansion.

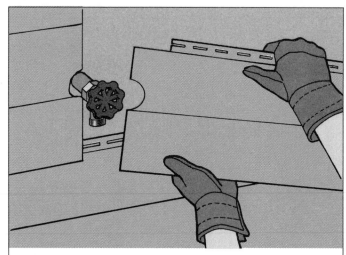

2 Cut the second panel, notching in an extra 1 in. for overlap.

Handling the Details

The small touches count when making a neat, weather-resistant job.

1 **Cutting for an Exterior Faucet.** Cut a joint in the piece of siding that bisects the faucet pipe. Use a utility knife to cut a half-round hole 1/4 inch wider than the pipe diameter. Fasten the piece in place.

2 **Fitting the Panel.** Cut a second panel, allowing an additional 1-inch overlap (for a total overlap of 1½ inch). Cut back the nail flange 1½ inches to allow for expansion.

3 **Sealing the Gap.** After nailing both pieces in place, use flexible sealant to seal the 1/4-inch gap around the faucet.

3 Fasten the pieces in place and use flexible sealant to caulk around the pipe.

Vertical Aluminum Siding

An important difference between aluminum and vinyl vertical siding is that aluminum does not require corner posts. The aluminum panels themselves are bent around the corner for a clean, weather-resistant covering.

As you reach a corner measure the horizontal distance to be covered at both the top and bottom of the panel, adding 1/8 inch to each. Clamp a board over the panel and align it with those points. Use another board to bend the piece over to make the corner.

Aluminum A lightweight, corrosion-resistant metal used for vertical and horizontal siding.

Blind nailing Nails driven so that the heads are concealed.

Building paper An asphalt-saturated felt or kraft paper installed behind siding to decrease air infiltration. Although it is waterproof, it also allows interior moisture to breathe outward. Synthetic wrapping material is used increasingly for this purpose.

Butt The bottom edge of a shingle or shake.

Caulking A soft compound used to seal joints against leaks (of water, air or noise). It may be silicone, neoprene, or one of a variety of other compounds.

Course A horizontal unit of shingles that runs the length of the wall.

Double coursing A method of applying wood shingles so that two complete layers of protection are provided at every course.

Eaves The edge of the roof that projects over the outside wall.

Exposure The portion of siding exposed to the weather; measured from the butt of one shingle to the butt of next course.

F-channel A type of trim used with synthetic siding; holds soffit panels.

Fascia Horizontal trim that covers the rafter ends at eaves.

Flashing A material used to prevent seepage of wind and water around intersections and projections on a wall.

Furring strips Construction-grade lumber that typically is ¾ inches in thickness; used to add depth or support, or as a nailing surface for siding.

Gable The triangular area of exterior wall created by the slope of a building's roof.

Hardboard A versatile wood by-product made of wood pulp pressed and adhered into sheets and planks.

Jamb The vertical inside face of a door or window opening.

J-channel Vinyl or aluminum siding trim used around windows and doors, and at eaves.

Lap The amount of siding covered by the overlap of the subsequent course of siding.

Nailer A strip of wood or a flange intended for fastening.

Shadow line The line of shadow caused by the thickness of a course of siding. This term typically is used when referring to shingles or shakes.

Shake A thick wooden shingle. There are four types: hand-split and resawn, taper-split, straight-split and taper-sawn.

Sheathing The wooden foundation of a wall; attached to wall studs as a solid surface behind the siding. Typically made of 1/2-inch construction-grade plywood or fiberboard, but older homes may have 3/4-inch shiplap or planks.

Shims Thin wood wedges used for tightening the fit between furring strips and a wall.

Soffit The finished underside of an eaves.

Square The number of bundles of shingles needed to cover 100 square feet.

Starter course The first course of siding; typically attached to a starter strip that is fastened at the base of a wall.

Starter strip A piece of furring or a vinyl or aluminum component necessary for installing the starter course.

Stepped flashing Flashing along a roof slope against a wall or chimney. It usually consists of L-shaped pieces of metal sheeting that fit into the joint behind the wall and over the roofing.

Story pole A site-made stick for determining course exposure.

Taper-split A wooden shake hand split from opposite ends of a block of wood.

Tongue and groove Planks that have a protruding tongue on one side and a groove (of the same size) on the other.

Undercoursing shingle Lower-grade wood shingles that typically have knots and irregular grain; used as a first layer in a starter course.

Vapor barrier A thin layer of moisture-resistant material that protects walls from interior household moisture. May be adhered to wallboard and insulation, or a separate sheet.

Vent An outlet for air. Such as a vent pipe in a plumbing system or a ventilating duct.

Vinyl A type of flexible water-and rot-resistant siding made from extruded polyvinyl chloride (PVC).

Weaving or Lacing Interweaving courses of wood shingles at outside or inside corners.

Z-flashing A piece of metal that resembles an expanded Z in profile. Used to shed water at the horizontal joint between two panels.